Conquering the Time Factor

Twelve Myths that Steal Life's Best Moments

Julie-Allyson Ieron

CHRISTIAN PUBLICATIONS, INC.

CAMP HILL, PENNSYLVANIA

✝CHRISTIAN PUBLICATIONS, INC.

3825 Hartzdale Drive, Camp Hill, PA 17011
www.christianpublications.com

Faithful, biblical publishing since 1883

Conquering the Time Factor
ISBN: 0-88965-213-9
© by Julie-Allyson Ieron
All rights reserved
Printed in the United States of America

02 03 04 05 06   5 4 3 2 1

Dedication

I offer this book, in gratitude, to my professors at Anderson and Ball State universities—Holly Miller, Helen Newell, Sandy Lovely, Hank Nuwer and especially Beverley Pitts—who imparted to me the ability and tenacity to communicate in writing those things that are closest to my heart.

And to Professor George Ramsey who drilled into me an intense passion to search the Bible for myself and keep at it until I found Truth.

Contents

Chapter 11

Chapter 12

Addendum

Acknowledgments

To my parents, John and Joyce Ieron, your continued patience with me and prayers for me throughout the writing of a book this year, of all years, qualify you for sainthood. I love and appreciate you both.

To my friends Jodi and Gail, how can I ever thank you for praying me through some of the most difficult seasons of this writing year? You'll never know how much I needed your support and encouragement.

To my publishers, especially to managing editor David Fessenden who encouraged me immeasurably by asking how soon I could have this book written so he could read it himself, to former editorial director George McPeek, to my editor Laurie Gustafson, to graphic artist Jerry Dorris who designed a cover that made you pick this book off the shelf and to the entire marketing team who saw to it that this book would make it into your hands—to each of you my undying gratitude for your partnership in this mission.

Finally, for you, my dear reader, I offer a prayer of thanksgiving that you've chosen to spend moments of your busy life reading what I've written. It is my hope that this book will challenge you, as its writing has challenged me, to personalize the psalmist's prayer:

> Teach me to do your will,
>   for you are my God;
> may your good Spirit
>   lead me on level ground.
>   (Psalm 143:10)

An Introductory Note

Dear Reader,

For several years now, my most requested speaking topic among groups across all age, gender and social lines continues to be my sometimes humorous and always practical presentation on time management titled, "I Can't Say 'No' & Other Time Management Myths." I've been invited to present it before such diverse groups as the Evangelical Press Association, Christian writer's conferences, denominational women's retreats and church-wide social events.

The reason this presentation and the topic of time management are so popular is that every one of us struggles with setting priorities, with establishing a pecking order in life, with deciding how to fit everything into the twenty-four hours we receive 365 times each year. Our time is painfully limited. Yet never have so many divergent voices called out to us, pleading or even demanding for us to spend our limited time and resources on their priorities. What we need is a reasoned response to this time dilemma. We need a response that will help us make *guilt-free* choices about how to use the hours set before us each new day. We need a response that will equip us to conquer the time factor each and every hour.

As I have spoken with individuals in my audiences, I've discovered that although our circumstances may differ, our struggles are remarkably similar. Most often these struggles boil down to a series of myths that life has fed us about how we *ought* to be using our time. Myths like:

- If I turn you down you'll think I don't value you, or worse, you'll be disappointed in me.

- I owe you a complete, satisfactory explanation when I choose not to do something.
- I'm selfish if I schedule time for myself.
- To accomplish a significant task, I must have a large, un-interrupted block of time and work straight through from start to finish.
- I must always make time for every interruption that comes across my path.
- I'm expected to be completely self-motivated, self-sufficient and self-directed.
- I'm responsible to meet every need of everyone at every time in every venue of my life.
- If I used to be able to make time for a task, I must always be able to make time for it.
- Rest, relaxation and retreating from the crowd are luxuries I'll never be able to afford.
- Those who scream the loudest need my attention the most.
- There is one set of priorities and one life pattern that every person must follow.
- True efficiency means I'm being wasteful of time or resources if I'm enjoying myself.

In this book I intend to help you debunk these myths. In so doing, I believe you will (as I have) find a workable perspective on ordering your own life. I feel the title *Conquering the Time Factor* aptly captures the essence of this book. The word *conquering* indicates that we have some positive control over our time use, and the word *factor* reminds us that time issues are a fact of life common to every one of us.

As you begin to gain control of your time usage through applying to each unique situation some of these helpful principles, you may choose to copy and complete the Periodic Self-Assessment Quiz I've included as an addendum to this book (see page 131). By using it on a bimonthly or semi-annual basis, it may prove to be a tool that will help you keep your life on track.

By the way, I have one confession to make. I approach life from the perspective of a fully convinced, fully sold-out follower of God and His Son, Jesus. So, my opinions on how I choose to order my life are indelibly stamped with this conviction. That's not meant to imply that the lessons I've learned don't apply to you if you do not share my conviction. In fact, many of my suggestions on time ordering apply to both men and women, both religious and secular and to those who share my faith and those who don't.

Whatever your convictions, I believe this book has something to offer to you. However—and I make no apologies here—I write what I have found to be true through my own experience. And what I've found to be true, above all else, are the wisdom, power, mercy and justice of God. I just wanted you to know that, going in.

I do not pretend to be an expert on time management, nor do I present myself as one who always applies the best principles of life ordering on a daily basis. But I am a fellow journeyer: one who has observed others, made mistakes herself and found a measure of hope for establishing a priority system that really works in everyday life. It is that hope and those lessons that I would like the privilege of sharing with you in the coming pages.

Thank you for spending a portion of your in-demand, highly valuable time with this book.

With my blessings,
Julie-Allyson Ieron

Myth: If I turn you down you'll think I don't value you,
or worse, you'll be disappointed in me.

I have a confession to make: I want you to like me. There, I
said it. It's a confession, and a matter of fact. I care what
you think of me. It's the way I'm wired.

Whether or not we would label ourselves "people pleasers"
by nature, it is my experience that every one of us cares what
other people—or at least *certain* other people—think of us. It
might look different depending upon our individual circumstances and stages of life, but each of us is playing life to an audience: bosses, spouses, parents, children, friends, colleagues,
church mates, classmates, etc.

Playing to an audience is fine . . . to a point. The problem is that
we tend to run into trouble when the different expectations and
demands these audience members place upon us conflict. We often find ourselves pushed and pulled between the expectations of
our families, our bosses or employees, our church—even our own
bodies. Attempting to consolidate it all can be utterly dizzying
and downright frustrating.

You and I aren't the only ones trying to balance external pressures as we make important choices. Not too long ago I watched
with interest a sequence of events surrounding President George
W. Bush. An avowed advocate of life, Mr. Bush was faced with a
highly publicized decision regarding government policy on stem
cell research. His closest advisors were bitterly divided. Media nail

5

biting went on for days as the public debated and awaited the president's decision. Eventually Mr. Bush announced a decision to allow medical research on the limited number of existing stem cells only. The fallout of this decision? Pro-lifers were angry at the use of fetal cells for any purpose, and the medical establishment was angry at the stringent limitations the small number placed upon their research. The president succeeded in pleasing virtually no one in his middle-ground decision.

> I can never please everyone with my choices
> in the area of how I spend the limited time
> I receive each day from the hand of God.

While the decisions we need to make from day to day may not take on the magnitude of President Bush's decision, I'm sure we can all relate with the principle to some degree.

Prescription for Trouble

At this point you're probably wondering why I have chosen to begin our discussion of conquering that tyrant—time—by refuting the myth that it is our obligation to please everyone whose opinion matters to us. I do so because I have found one fact to be irrevocably true: I can never please everyone with my choices in the area of how I spend the limited time I receive each day from the hand of God. If I say yes to one opportunity, I am obligated (for the sake of my health and sanity) to say no to dozens of other worthy and good ones. Then, for every one person temporarily pleased with me, dozens of others are at least temporarily disappointed with me.

I used to think (or at least act as if) my body were constructed of the same indestructible material as a cartoon character. Bend me, I won't break; leave me dangling in midair without a safety net and I'll sprout wings to fly myself to safety. Back in the dark ages when I was a twenty-year-old graduate student, I felt invincible. Sleep? Who needed it? So many opportunities to gain experience in my career field surrounded me that I felt the need to grab every one of them.

At one point I was juggling a full-time class schedule, a supposedly part-time job that demanded a forty-hour-a-week commitment, writing duties at three magazines and a newspaper, choir and orchestra rehearsals at my church (thirty miles from campus) and a comfortably pleasant dating relationship. When my friends wanted a place to gather, I was the happy hostess. When my boyfriend offered tickets to a sold-out show in nearby Indianapolis, I was ready to go. When my boss needed me to teach her undergraduate classes while she was away, I was happy to oblige. When an editor called to offer a hot article tip, I followed up with gritty tenacity.

For one glittering moment, everyone was pleased with me. It was a heady, albeit short-lived, hurrah.

However, it didn't take too many months of existing on catnaps and nutrition bars for my body to rebel. My first moment of clarity amid the blur of people pleasing came when I found myself in the university hospital emergency room, where my alarmed friends brought me after a simple flu bug ran roughshod over my worn down body. The insightful prescription of the on-duty resident? Go home and rest. No talking. No working. Just rest—for as long as it takes.

Out of options, I rested. My boss was disappointed. My editors stopped calling. My professors weren't necessarily inclined to extend project due dates. The orchestra director couldn't understand why I resigned from the violin section. To his credit, my boyfriend was understanding. But most of the others who just days before had been singing my praises were scrambling to locate new and able victims—uh, volunteers.

The Right Questions

Through that painful experience of conquering the time factor I began to learn the truth: I'm not designed to please everyone. It is a realization which begs the question: *If I'm not made to please everyone, what* am *I made to do?* I realized that was the question I should have been asking all along.

As I do with all of the big questions of life, I turned to the Bible in search of answers. To my amazement, I found the Bible harbors distinct and powerful words on the subject. Specifically, I found Ephesians 2:10, where Paul writes: "For we are God's workmanship, created in Christ Jesus to do good works, which God prepared in advance for us to do."

Each day God prepares a day's worth of work for me; likewise, each day He prepares *me* for the work.

I'd always held to a nebulous notion that God has a plan for me; I'd assumed, though, that it would come to me in a one-time, life-encompassing revelation. However, as I read those words in Ephesians, I saw with newly enlightened eyes that not only does God have a big-picture dream for me, but He has mapped out work for me to do. Daily work. Or, more to the point, one-day-at-a-time work. Each day God prepares a day's worth of work for me; likewise, each day He prepares *me* for the work. It stands to reason, then, that for the follower of God the dilemma of which audience to please is moot. The only audience I need to please is the Creator who made me for the work and the work for me.

In my mind this raised the question of whether, when He created the plan, He would have taken into account my health concerns, my limitations as one time-bound human on this globe, my gifts and abilities and heart cries. Even as I tried to form the question of whether or not an all-powerful, supernatural God could ever relate to my frailty, I recalled these words, penned by another letter writer in the Bible:

> For we do not have a high priest who is unable to sympathize with our weaknesses, but we have one who has been tempted in every way, just as we are—yet was without sin. Let us then approach the throne of grace with confidence, so that we may receive mercy and find grace to help us in our time of need. (Hebrews 4:15-16)

Referred to in Hebrews as the "high priest," Jesus laid aside all of the privileges of deity in part so that we would know that He is able to "sympathize with our weaknesses." That word "our" means mine and yours. Several years ago, I heard author and songwriter Gloria Gaither explain it this way: "Jesus didn't come to Earth to find out what it was like to be one of us; He came to let us know that He has always known." I can still hear Gloria speak that phrase in an emphatic whisper: "He has *always* known." That precise truth has been a source of immeasurable comfort and encouragement to me through many of the inevitable difficult seasons of life.

Similarly, listen for the comforting words the prophet Isaiah records exactly as God spoke them:

> Do you not know?
>   Have you not heard?
> The LORD is the everlasting God,
>   the Creator of the ends of the earth.
> He will not grow tired or weary,
>   and his understanding no one can fathom.
> He gives strength to the weary

and increases the power of the weak.
Even youths grow tired and weary,
    and young men stumble and fall;
but those who hope in the LORD
    will renew their strength.
They will soar on wings like eagles;
    they will run and not grow weary,
        they will walk and not be faint. (Isaiah 40:28-31)

As I stopped to process the implications of this truth, it finally jelled in my mind that the only one I need to worry about pleasing is the One who designed a specific, doable plan for each moment of my life, who has the idiosyncrasies of my specific makeup firmly in hand. He has an understanding no one else could approach. And when I'm about the business He has prepared for me, He will provide more than sufficient strength to accomplish the task.

Do you have any idea how freeing this principle was for a worn-out people pleaser like I was?

From Theory to Practice

As with all concepts drawn from the pages of Scripture, this principle of pleasing God and God alone with the choices I make in my daily life seemed at once simple and, at the same time, unattainable. It sounded great in theory—I mean, of course I'm willing to set aside the desires of everyone except God—but two problems began to surface as I tried to put the theory into practice.

Problem one came up when I tried to determine exactly which works God had created for me to accomplish each day. Unfortunately, in this time and place in history God seldom speaks as audibly and clearly as He did to Isaiah or Moses or Abraham or the disciples. So we are left to search His Bible for the big-picture answers and to listen for the still small voice of His Holy Spirit giving us subtle nudges through Scripture, through circumstances and through trusted advisors, pastors and teachers. It requires silence, attentiveness, teachability, a trained ear and a healthier dose of patience than I often have on hand.

That issue aside, though, problem two grows out of the solutions to problem one. Once we are convinced that God is leading us to say yes to this or that opportunity, or no to another, we have little hard evidence that would convince anyone else of the verity of our interpretation of God's direction. From a purely human standpoint, there are certain "others"—be they family, spouse or employer—whose demands upon us we cannot ignore. Likewise, if we do choose to set aside someone else's desires to follow God's direction, we take the real risk that we will alienate that person and therefore bear substantial consequences.

This too is a lesson I learned painfully. I am self-employed, and I work diligently to please my clients. Consulting, writing and editing fees pay my bills. It is in my best interest to keep serving my clients' whims and desires. Unfortunately, this is not always possible. About a year ago one of my largest clients called with a lucrative offer of a large writing project. I compared the deadline to the others already on my job log and found that although it would be a tight squeeze, the job would be doable. Even as I agreed to meet with the client and other project team members, however, I began to feel an unnamed, nagging concern.

After the meeting I sought candid counsel with other knowledgeable players. As I prayed about my participation in the project, my internal alarms escalated in intensity. Soon I knew I was the wrong person to take on the project. I wondered whether I could be in my right mind to turn down such a lucrative offer, particularly from this client. Yet, despite my misgivings about the business sense of my decision, I recognized that I had to be true to what I knew to be God's leading.

So, I called the client, expressed my concerns and turned down the project. The client said he understood and actually validated my concerns. He said he'd keep me in mind for other projects. I haven't heard from him even once since then.

Saying No with Confidence

When I said no, someone else said yes, and the proposal was no longer open to me. It didn't take me long to come to the conclusion that I'd be squandering resources if I were to obsess about whether or not I'd made the right call.

Despite science fiction hypotheses to the contrary, part of being human means we do not have the ability to turn back time one year, one week, one hour, even one minute. A decision, once made, can seldom be revisited or changed. This leads me to another affirming, biblical concept: Yes means yes and no means no. We'll get more into this principle in the next chapter, but for now, consider these words spoken by Jesus in His most famous sermon: "Simply let your 'Yes' be 'Yes,' and your 'No,' 'No'" (Matthew 5:37). In other words, when I say yes, I commit to follow through, to throw all of my resources, energies and attention into a project. But when I say no, I'm not playing games. To me, "no" doesn't mean that I really want someone to beg me or massage my ego or guilt trip me into doing something. Instead, it means this is not right for me to do, even though it may indeed be a good thing for someone else. It may mean that it doesn't fit into my goals and objectives; or, it is not the right time for me to undertake it; or, it would siphon resources away from something that is higher on the list of priorities I've set prayerfully, with God's direction. Whatever the reason, no means no.

I look to the earthly life and ministry of Jesus Christ as my life example. His Father set before Him the greatest task in all human history—the crucial purpose of saving us from our own sins and restoring our relationship with our Creator. Jesus ordered His limited years of walking this earth in such a way that when the shadow of the cross was looming largest on His horizon, He was able to say with confidence, "[Father,] I have finished the work which You have given Me to do" (John 17:4, NKJV).

> I cannot please God while trying to coerce someone into taking on responsibilities He has designed for me; nor can I please Him by being vain enough to think I can shoulder someone else's portion of His work.

It intrigues me to note that although Jesus successfully and completely accomplished His calling—there is nothing we could add to or subtract from this finished work—He left the church with the ongoing task of ministry in the world. The whole church. We are *each* responsible for the task He established for us. I for mine; you for yours. Together with His people of all generations, we will accomplish the task set before us—together, not a handful of us firing as loose cannons on our own.

Implied in the acknowledgment of this truth is the fact that I cannot please God while trying to coerce someone into taking on responsibilities He has designed for me; nor can I please Him by being vain enough to think I can shoulder someone else's portion of His work. We can cheer other believers on, but we can't do their work for them.

This principle has been especially helpful as I've sought to replace the income and rebuild my client base in the wake of turning down that project. Before making the momentous decision to turn down that project, I had taken time to gather the facts. I spoke to trusted advisors, I prayed, I did all I knew to do.

Not fully understanding the consequences, yet convinced of God's direction, I made the difficult choice to trust God's direction. I was helped by acknowledging that while He did not call me to this task, if He wanted it accomplished, He would call someone else. The accomplishment of the task was out of my hands—which is to say it was in God's hands, where it's always been. Overall, that's not a bad place to be.

Challenge of the Week

Read as much of the Gospels (Matthew, Mark, Luke and John) as you can, looking for signs that point to the choices Jesus Christ made about how He spent His time on earth. Note the amount of time He spent teaching His followers, healing hurting people and getting alone with His Father. Note His frustration with those whose priorities were not aligned with His Father's. Record all of your observations in a journal or in the space below.

Myth: I owe you a complete, satisfactory explanation
when I choose not to do something.

My apologies to the men reading this book, but I ask
your indulgence as I share a "female" story. I call this a
female story because I've never known men to get themselves into
these predicaments—at least not quite this way. Here's what I
mean.

A couple of years ago friends invited my mom and me to a
party at their home. It was a demonstration party—where a
woman employed part-time as an in-home sales representative
demonstrates how to use a line of products. In the process, she
invites guests to not only purchase the products (if they buy
enough, the hostesses receive a slew of free gifts), but also to
host parties in their own homes.

The products were nice—a bit pricey, but nice. It was not
guilt alone that caused me to make a few select purchases to give
as Christmas gifts. This was not the first demonstration party I
had attended (I knew what to expect when I accepted the invita-
tion); nor was it to be the last. In fact, I'm considering hosting
one for another product line (with another demonstrator) in
the not-too-distant future.

It was as I was in line preparing to write my check that I overheard the conversation that troubled me.

Demonstrator: Thank you for your purchase.
Guest: Yes, these are lovely products.

Demonstrator: Aren't they, though? Wouldn't you like to host a party in your home? Think of all of the cool stuff you could get for free.

Guest: I'd like to, but I'm just so busy. Sorry.

Demonstrator: Aren't we all? Well, I can help you out. Just give me a list and I'll send out all the invitations.

Guest: Thanks, but I'd want to do it up right, and I just don't have time to get everything ready when I come home from work.

Demonstrator: I'll be happy to pick up some chips and dip to serve as treats. I'll even come by early to help you run the vacuum or dust the family room. Whatever you need.

Guest: Well, uh, that's nice of you, but it's not a convenient time right now. We're remodeling the bathroom this month.

Demonstrator: No problem at all. I have plenty of dates available next month. How about the 27th or the 29th?

Guest: Well, um, I guess the 29th will be fine.

The demonstrator got the guest to commit to hosting a party when she didn't want to. How did she do it? She had a rehearsed answer for every excuse the guest could make. (Remember: Not every demonstrator uses these high-pressure tactics, so don't be overly leery of attending one of these parties.)

I was next in line. Now, I teach audiences to avoid being pressured into doing something that doesn't fit into their goals and objectives. We'd soon see whether I could practice what I teach.

Demonstrator: Thank you for your purchase.

I nod silently, smiling slightly.

Demonstrator: You know, you could get a lot more great products if you host a party in your home. Let me put you down for a date.

Me: Thanks for offering, but no thank you.

Demonstrator: Why not? It would be great.

Me: I'm sure it would, but no.
Demonstrator: Oh, c'mon. Don't you want your friends to
see these great products?
Me: I can't, but thank you anyway.

When she saw I wouldn't be coerced into playing into her script, she lost interest. I suppressed an amused grin as I realized that without an excuse from me, the woman with all the answers was at a loss.

Normally, I'm open and honest to a fault. As one who cares about what others think, I want to let them know I'm not devaluing them or their request, and that I'm not turning them down without good reason. But this demonstrator was not my boss, my employee, my parent, my spouse or even my friend. Her behavior, in fact, made it imperative for me to offer no explanation. With her, I felt rather like the exhausted parent of an inquisitive two-year-old, worn down by a thousand "why" inquiries, who finally resorts to "because I said so" or "because that's the way it is" to procure a moment's peace.

My object was not to frustrate the demonstrator; but it was to do what we discussed in the last chapter: let my yes be yes and my no be no. If I'd tried to tell this woman, "No, because of this or that reason," she'd have had me for lunch. It had to be no—period—no reason, no excuse, just no.

My reasons for turning down the opportunity the demonstrator offered were personal, fixed and not up for discussion. Hostessing a party for my friends or colleagues did not at that time rank on the priority list of those things around which I had ordered my life. So, I said a firm and nonnegotiable "no."

Ordering vs. Management

You may have already noted that I like to refer to getting our schedules and lives under control as "time ordering" rather than "time management." This slight verbal adjustment paints a valuable picture for us to consider.

> If we expect to become time's master we will be sorely disillusioned, perhaps even tempted to give up on trying to control our use of this most valuable of resources.

The word "management" implies that time is something I can command, beat into shape and control. I earned a degree in management, and over the years I've had opportunity to put a lot of good management principles into practice in the work world. Yet I have not found a way to direct time as I would a department made up of various employees. As we'll discuss in later chapters, when it comes to time demands, outside factors may dictate our actions for us. If we expect to become time's master we will be sorely disillusioned, perhaps even tempted to give up on trying to control our use of this most valuable of resources.

Conversely, the word "ordering" puts me in mind of someone moving into a new home—perhaps because I am doing just that in the midst of writing this book. As I empty each box, I make conscious decisions on where to place items. I place those things I use every day at eye level, nearer to the front of cabinets, drawers and closets than those things I use infrequently. For example, adhesive bandages and first-aid ointments occupy the prime spots in my medicine cabinet, because when I need them, I need them *right now*. (If you knew what a klutz I am, you'd understand why first-aid products are a priority for me.)

Priorities Are Key

If you noticed the phrase "time ordering" cropping up in these first two chapters, you're likely also to have noticed that I keep referring to "knowing my priorities." I contend that we cannot begin to order our use of time without first knowing what is important to us at our current stage of life and without recognizing which items and concerns ought to be placed up front, at eye level.

The first article I ever had published (in my college newspaper) was on the subject of prioritizing. I can recall the editor arguing with me that "prioritize" was not a dictionary-recognized word. She accused me of "verbing" (making a noun into a verb), a cardinal sin for the budding writer. I must have been ahead of my time, though, because in the last decade or so, as our lives have become more complex, "prioritize" has become a dreaded but universally recognized word. I located it in my electronic version of The American Heritage Dictionary this morning, defined as: "To arrange or deal with in order of importance."

As a follower of Christ, my first order of importance is to please and honor Him. So, the best of my time and energies is spent on prayer, Scripture reading and on bringing Him praise through my actions and my words. If you were to initiate a search of my electronic planner for items relating to my faith, you'd find several relevant categories. Among them are Bible passages to remember, prayer lists, church-related activities and sermon notes, to name a few. The frequency of these elements as they occur in my daily and weekly schedules would indicate to anyone reading over my shoulder that I place a high priority on things related to my faith.

Other priorities I hold at this season of my life include getting our builder to complete my new suite so I can complete my move; writing this book; meeting the needs and expectations of my family; spending time with the single adults group at church where I am a leader; preparing well to teach my students at the Bible college this semester; building my writing, consulting and speaking business despite turbulent economic times; promoting the three books I've already published; establishing and maintaining healthy relationships with friends, colleagues and extended family; and keeping my body and mind refreshed.

God has mapped out work for each of us to do.

I have intentionally listed these priorities out of order for two reasons: First, the way I order mine will differ from the way you order yours, and I don't want to hold my priorities up as the one and only right pattern you must use to set your priorities; second, different seasons of life require intentional and thoughtful adjustments in the order. For example, as my moving day nears, packing boxes and cajoling the builder into making the final few adjustments have moved ahead of completing this book. Similarly, on weeks when I am booked for a speaking engagement or a media appearance to promote a book, preparation for those matters takes priority over having dinner with a friend. The key here is to make these decisions intentionally, rather than to allow events to dictate my choices by default.

But among the myriad choices, how can we decide what is more important and what is less important? While no one can dictate the proper pattern for you, I do have an informed opinion on how you can create one for yourself. It harkens back to the key principle discussed in the previous chapter: namely, that God has mapped out work for each of us to do. If this is true, then as we set our priorities it would seem most profitable for us to prayerfully approach Him and search His Word for our answers.

After prayer I located two Bible verses that best state my big-picture, overarching life priority; I'd recommend that you search the Bible for yourself to find verses that best state God's direction for you. Mine are found in Proverbs 3:5-6. I carry them with me in my planner, personalized to fit my situation. The paraphrase I carry reads, "I will trust in the Lord with all my heart and will not depend on my limited understanding. In everything I do I will put God first and trust Him to place me on a straight path." Knowing this to be my ultimate priority, I can then measure every other aspect of my life—every other element of my schedule—with that in mind. It helps me translate the theoretical into the practical.

For example, God has called and equipped me to be a writer, so I make every effort as I write both secular and faith-based projects to be God-honoring in my writing. Likewise, when I made the difficult decision to turn down the big project I mentioned earlier, I did so not depending on my limited understanding but trusting the guidance God made plain to me.

Without this valuable, overarching principle to guide and measure each choice I make, I am afraid I would flounder in the sea of indecision or by default allow my choices to be made by others who may not have my best interests at heart.

Gentle, but Firm

How does this priority setting relate back to how we answer those who try to sidetrack us or to convince us to do things that we know we would be misguided to attempt? Let's look to the example of Jesus in His earthly ministry to find the answer. If you took the "Challenge of the Week" at the conclusion of the first chapter, you'll likely be able to identify the overarching purpose of Jesus' earthly life. Jesus states it near the end of His time on this planet when He says, "[Father,] I have brought you glory on earth by completing the work you gave me to do" (John 17:4). He also states it early on, as a twelve-year-old boy in response to His parents' concern for His well-being: "Did you not know that I must be about My Father's business?" (Luke 2:49, NKJV).

Mary and Joseph, careful to follow the letter of Jewish law, caravan from Nazareth to Jerusalem with friends and family members to celebrate the Passover feast. The city is awash in festivities and inundated with celebrants visiting from across the Jewish world. After participating in the Passover, the caravan begins its journey home. The mood is celebratory. For an entire day no one notices that the party is one member smaller than it was on the journey to Jerusalem. Suddenly, Mary and Joseph realize that Jesus is nowhere to be found. In a panic they rush back to the city. (How do you explain to God that you've *lost* His Son?) It takes them another two days, but they finally locate Him. What is He doing? He is seated in the temple among the teachers listening to them and asking questions of them.

Mary is beside herself, demanding an answer to why her perfect son would put her through these days of agony. Jesus' response is direct and matter-of-fact, but not overly explanatory. In essence: "I'm doing what I'm supposed to be doing—the work of My Father." The unspoken implication is this: "Mother, you wouldn't want to stand in the way of My accomplishing God's work, would you?"

Bible commentator Matthew Henry explains it this way: "It becomes the children of God, in conformity to Christ, to attend their heavenly Father's business, and to make all other business give way to it."[1]

The People Factor

Jesus offers His answer to Mary by way of explanation, but not excuse. Although some dictionary definitions do not make a distinction between the two, it might be helpful for us to recognize the nuances of both terms in common usage. An *explanation* is nonnegotiable. It simply describes the reasons for an action. "I was about My Father's business"—period, end of discussion.

On the other hand, most often an *excuse* offers reasons with the express intent of *justifying* one's actions. It is a subtle, but important, difference. If I'm trying to justify myself to you, I am giving you power to validate or invalidate my choices. If I simply offer an explanation (abbreviated or detailed), I am stating a matter of fact that is unchanging regardless of your attitudes toward my decision.

As Jesus modeled for us, we are wise to subordinate all other matters to the calling God has placed upon our lives. Once we are persuaded that we have prioritized our lives properly, the need for the approval of outsiders carries less weight. There is no longer any excuse for excuses. Explanations can be useful, but excuses are out.

If I'm trying to justify myself to you, I am giving you power to validate or invalidate my choices.

I like the way the apostles Peter and John demonstrate this concept as they explain the necessity of their work to an angry assembly of religious leaders who were demanding that they stop speaking publicly about Jesus: "Judge for yourselves whether it is right in God's sight to obey you rather than God" (Acts 4:19).

Some people in our lives have earned the right to an explanation—either during a situation or after the fact. Sometimes I'll say to my mother (who is my best friend and an invaluable volunteer assistant in my business), "Just trust me; I'll explain later." She respects me enough for this explanation to be sufficient. When I do offer more detail, she will affirm me, hold me accountable, perhaps ask a question, but she will not attempt to derail me. Similarly, I can tell her, "Mom, I'm spent; I've been at my computer for ten hours straight; can we do your project another day?" And she will empathize rather than exerting additional pressure.

It is helpful to remember, though, that sometimes even with our closest loved ones or highest earthly authorities, it is sufficient and necessary to remind them succinctly that we have set our priorities and we will not be sidetracked. We are, after all, about our Father's business.

Challenge of the Week

From God's perspective, it may not always be in our best interests to know the complete answer of why He acts in certain ways or allows events to unfold as they do. Skim through the Old Testament book of Job this week. Pay particular attention to chapters 38 through 42. Consider the questions Job asks of God. Then note how God chooses to answer. Is there any evidence that Job comes to know the real reason (see Job 1) for his trials? Ask yourself why Job finds God's response sufficient, and record your thoughts below or in a journal.

Endnote

1. *Matthew Henry's Commentary on the Whole Bible*, Electronic Edition: Luke 2:41-52, p. 17.

Myth: I'm selfish if I schedule time for myself.

In Christian circles we tend to take to the farthest extreme the concept of placing others' needs ahead of our own—to the point where we consider taking care of ourselves to be a less desirable (maybe even sinful) way to spend our energies. However, upon close examination of His earthly life we see that Jesus modeled both self-sacrifice and self-preservation. He sacrificed Himself by laying aside His privileges as King of the Universe to become a man, and then laid down His life in our place, but He also recognized the need to take care of His Father's gift of life and health.

I am amazed at the number of times in the four Gospels that Jesus is either described as "going alone" or quoted as instructing His followers to do the same. Here is but a partial list:

- Matthew 14:23-24—"After he [Jesus] had dismissed them, he went up on a mountainside by himself to pray. When evening came, he was there alone."

- Mark 6:31-32—"Then, because so many people were coming and going that they did not even have a chance to eat, he said to them, 'Come with me by yourselves to a quiet place and get some rest.' So they went away by themselves in a boat to a solitary place."

- Mark 6:47—"When evening came, the boat was in the middle of the lake, and he [Jesus] was alone on land."

- Mark 9:2—"After six days Jesus took Peter, James and John with him and led them up a high mountain, where they were all alone."
- John 6:15—"Jesus, knowing that they intended to come and make him king by force, withdrew again to a mountain by himself."

Going alone plays a critical role in our continued usefulness for the tasks to which He has called us.

The sheer number of times this phrase occurs in reports of Jesus' life is an indication to me that going alone—taking time apart from all of the activity of everyday life and even away from the hard work of ministry—plays a critical role in our continued usefulness for the tasks to which He has called us.

It occurs to me, as I read these verses in context, that times of active work need to be followed by times of quiet. The scene from Mark 6:31-32 quoted above, for example, records Jesus calling the disciples aside to rest after they have come back from intense missionary trips. I also see that some of the best ministry comes during or after times of quiet. In Mark 9 Jesus takes His inner circle aside so they can see Him transfigured in all His glory. Without quiet times we may not be still enough, attentive enough or attuned enough to catch a glimpse of the awesome nature of the God we serve.

Julie's Journal: A Very Bad Day

That's all good in theory, but what about in practice? I'm a single adult, so I'm supposed to have tons of discretionary time—more than my friends who are juggling work and husbands and children. I have found, however, that even *I* don't seem to be able to find the time to do things I enjoy, like practicing my violin or stenciling the guest bathroom or having a long talk on the telephone with a good friend.

Several years ago, as I was preparing to present "I Can't Say 'No' & Other Time Management Myths" as a speech for the first time, I began feeling pretty cocky about my time choices and all the good counsel I could offer to my listeners. Just then, this atypical Wednesday hit and knocked me right off my high perch and back into the real world. It's a day I've shared with every audience since, one that brings nods of ascent and whispers of understanding.

The alarm went off at 5:29 a.m., as it has every weekday since I began commuting to work. I listened to the 5:38 traffic report before I forced back the covers.

Between 5:39 and 6:15 I made breakfast for my dad and myself, showered, dressed, packed my lunch, made tea for my mom who had the flu and cleaned up the dishes. I backed the car out of the driveway right at 6:15, so I beat the two trains I would have encountered at the railroad tracks if I had left at 6:16. This saved fifteen minutes.

It took thirty-five minutes to get downtown, so I found myself playing ring-around-the-parking-garage at 6:50. That meant I got to park on level 3.5—"only" seven rings up. At 6:55 I arrived at my desk, desperate for another coffee. I checked e-mail, voice mail and snail mail (what we all used to know as mail a few years ago), which took an hour. Three mails instead of one—how enlightened we are.

At 7:55 I called my sick grandmother to be sure she had enough cough medicine and chicken soup; she had to take off her hearing aid before she could hear me. The call took four minutes. This left just enough time to grab my fourth cup of coffee before dashing off to the conference room for a meeting.

The meeting ran long, and I emerged two hours later with a list of eighteen new tasks to complete. When I got to my desk, I found an urgent message from a supplier; we called an emergency meeting.

At 11:29 my lunch appointment arrived, so I sent my secretary to let the client through the security doors, because the emergency meeting was starting at 11:30. We made quick decisions because everyone was hungry (note: this is a good time for a meeting), and I was on my way to my luncheon by 11:45. We ate and discussed business simultaneously.

At 1 p.m., I returned to my desk to do the work I was supposed to have finished B.C. (before crisis). I answered more messages, checked e-mail, wrote and read and drank twice-reheated coffee. I checked eight items off my list, leaving a net increase of ten items more than I'd had on the list at 6:55 that morning.

By the time I was ready to reverse the ring-around-the-parking-garage game, the radio traffic reporter was saying, "Forget about the gas pedal; get that braking foot ready."

It took one hour and twenty-five minutes to get home. While in the car, I returned phone calls and listened to a tape I agreed to review for a magazine. Mostly I fumed.

At 5 o'clock I pulled into my garage spot, changed clothes, gave Mom her medicine and started cooking dinner. I decided to make a vegetable stir fry. But Dad wanted meat and potatoes (the only member of his vegetable universe is the inimitable corn—which I detest). Mom said, "Wouldn't soup be nice?" I boiled chicken, vegetables and Mom's favorite little noodles while I was preparing Dad's steak, potatoes and corn and my stir fry. I poured a bowl of the steaming yellow liquid for Mom and carried it to her room on a tray. In her congested state she took one sniff, wrinkled her nose and announced that the soup smelled terrible. Couldn't she have something else to eat? I wanted to cry. My food got cold.

After I got everyone fed, it was nearly 9 p.m. I still had bills to pay and a dishwasher to run and empty. At 9:30 I decided to get a jump on the morning by setting the table and the coffeemaker for breakfast. At 9:45 I collapsed.

So much for being a time management guru; I couldn't gain control of one little, pesky day.

Setting a Schedule

At first I wondered whether I was alone in experiencing these chaotic and demanding days. As I searched my local library database to see how popular magazines were describing the time-related concerns modern men and women are encountering, I realized I am not alone. In fact, I found articles with titles like "The Overwhelmed Person's Guide to Time Management" (this I understand, because I often feel breathless and overwhelmed); "Beating the Clock" (there are some days when I feel like beating a clock, but I don't think that's what they had in mind); and "Time Shifting: Creating More Time to Enjoy Life" (as far as I know, only One can *create* time—and I am not He).

The most telling article I found appeared in the March 1997 issue of *Parenting* magazine. Titled "A Toddler's Date Book," it was a review of a colorful planner that comes with cute little stickers and activities to make scheduling fun for a tot. Now, out of necessity I've become a strong advocate of adults carrying a date book or calendar and a to-do list with us wherever we go. But a *toddler's* date book? At first I wondered whether we aren't starting them a little young—let a kid be a kid, you know? Then again, perhaps good planning habits established at a young age will translate into well-ordered, productive years as an adult.

One of the biggest helps in getting a handle on ordering my time is a handy little object I carry with me wherever I go (even on the occasional dinner date). It is my planner. I've recently transitioned from a ten-ton leather planner with hundreds of loose-leaf pages to a six-ounce electronic organizer that is truly amazing. On it I keep a record of all of my appointments, a to-do list, a log file containing comments on all of the projects I'm under contract to write, a separate log to track speaking engagements, another to track book sales, note files on each chapter of this book and more. I also keep files of Scripture promises and sermon notes, and a complete e-book Bible in the gadget's memory.

The first time I learned to make use of a planner was when I was a college freshman. I was carrying twenty hours of classes and was responsible to seven instructors plus my private violin teacher. As the syllabi started to fill my notebook the first week of classes, I realized that only with a plan could I get every project completed on time. I laid out the syllabi on a table, side by side with my shiny new day planner. One by one I began to note the due dates of each paper and exam; many were due within hours of each other. So, I backtracked through the weeks preceding those deadlines to plan when I'd need to research each project, when each paper needed to be completed (my deadline, not my professor's) and when I'd need to study for each exam. That semester, despite complications added by my father's life-threatening illness, I was able to complete every project on time and come away with a GPA that made my parents proud. I had my day planner to thank for that success. I've been a planner junkie ever since.

More sophisticated but no less sold on the concept today, I regularly consult all of the files I keep in my planner's memory. However, the calendar with its alarm-reminders and pop-up daily schedule is the most valuable tool in the kit. I love entrusting my schedule to this little assistant. When asked to attend a meeting, I can blame the organizer if I can't make it. "Sorry, I have another appointment scheduled for that day/time." No more double booking. No more over-committing. No more forgetting to be where I've promised I'd be or to make the phone call I've promised to make. This little gadget keeps me on time and less frazzled, making it easier and more fun to take care of my body's need for work and rest times.

> ## If I don't block out the time well in advance, work will multiply and fill the hours I'd intended to spend as rest time.

Why do I include a high-pressure pitch for day planners in a chapter on taking care of ourselves? As I try to take care of myself, I find I need an assistant to guard my time and remind me of my priorities. Since I can't afford to employ a twenty-four-hour-a-day personal executive assistant, my electronic scheduler fills that role, allowing me to schedule down time, project time and uninterrupted writing time, without feeling guilty. I literally put social events and quiet times right on the calendar, side by side with due dates and client meetings. I find that if I schedule time for myself, I will take it. Conversely, if I don't block out the time well in advance, work will multiply and fill the hours I'd intended to spend as rest time.

The Necessity of Getting Alone

Rest times are as old as the first week of this world's history. Following six days of creating the universe, God did what? He rested. It is a pattern He prescribed for His people to follow when He gave the Ten Commandments to Moses on the mountain. Work for six days; on the seventh, take a breather. On a practical level, sometimes taking care of myself means getting away, getting alone, stepping off the track long enough to catch my breath.

Many of my friends who are parents of toddlers use the concept of "time out" as a discipline technique. A six-year-old misbehaving while his mother is talking on the telephone trembles when his mommy demands, "Do you need a time-out?" He stops whining or jumping or throwing food at his baby sister for fear that he'll be sent to sit still and quiet, away from toys, TV and companionship.

It's a shame that we've come to consider time-out a punishment. In our home, we use it as a safety valve. I've learned that when I arrive home after speaking at a retreat or spending a twelve-hour day writing or driving through a two-hour commute, it may be the wisest thing I can do to announce to the family, "I need a time-out."

I'll go into the bedroom, start the Jacuzzi tub, turn on a mellow CD and spend time calming down, settling back, loosening tight neck muscles, rubbing throbbing temples and talking the day over with my heavenly Father. When I've taken sufficient time to do this, I am a more sociable daughter, better equipped to respond to issues of concern at home than when I stormed into the house minutes or hours before.

Do I have the luxury of taking a time-out every time I'm stressed? Unfortunately not. But I do make every effort to create niches for time out during times of high stress. Even if creating a niche means nothing more than making a conscious attitude adjustment. For example, in the Wednesday I described earlier, the only alone time I had was when I was stuck in traffic. As my foot was firmly pressed on the brake pedal, my mind was firmly entrenched in its fuming and fussing mode. I needed a time-out, if only in my own mind. I needed to do what a doctor friend of mine calls, "telling Father on 'em all." When she is feeling trapped, she drags all her complaints to God and dumps them in His lap. As she entrusts frustrations into His hands, she finds herself relieved and comforted.

> ## Our reward of God's presence and favor comes when we are alone and pouring our hearts out to Him in secret.

There have been other rainy Wednesdays when I have found myself similarly in need of relief and comfort. When I've shut off the car stereo (or turned on a peaceful tape) and carried my concerns and complaints to God, I've been more peaceful, more in control by the time I reached home.

Are We Really Alone?

This concept does work, and for a good reason. Jesus explains it to His disciples hours before going to the cross. "But a time is coming, and has come, when you will be scattered, each to his own home. *You will leave me all alone. Yet I am not alone, for my Father is with me.* I have told you these things, so that in me you may have peace" (John 16:32-33).

Jesus asks His followers to take comfort and peace in the middle of troubled times by remembering that even when we feel the most abandoned, we are not alone, for our Father is with us. In fact, it is when we are alone that we are ushered into God's throne room. Listen to Jesus' instructions to us: "But when you pray, go into your room, close the door and pray to your Father, who is unseen. Then your Father, who sees what is done in secret, will reward you" (Matthew 6:6). Our reward of His presence and favor comes when we are alone and pouring our hearts out to Him in secret.

All of these truths remind me that scheduling time to be alone with my thoughts and with my God is neither selfish nor self-serving. Rather it is a necessary way to spend my time—a requirement built into the very fiber of God's creation.

Challenge of the Week

Consider the divine appointment Jesus had with the Samaritan woman in John 4:1-42. Clearly weary from His journey, Jesus was taking well-earned time apart from the crowds. However, in the midst of His rest, He took time to minister to this woman. Think about how Jesus spent His "vacation" in the town of Sychar. How did His activities there fit into what you know to be true of His goals and priorities? If you've taken time to set your life goal and establish your priorities, examine your own schedule to see how well each appointment on your calendar fits into your overall life purpose. Journal your thoughts.

Myth: To accomplish a significant task, I must have a large, uninterrupted block of time and work straight through from start to finish.

For the next two chapters, we're going to cover interruptions—or more specifically how to conquer them before they conquer us. We all have them—every day. And if we are to keep them from derailing our agendas and obliterating our well-set goals, we need a battle plan.

Procrastination is one kind of interruption—a self-induced kind of interruption, where our own desire to put off a task interrupts the job's completion. I would define procrastination as allowing things within our control to manipulate us into not doing what we know we ought to be doing. In this chapter, we'll work on ways to get a healthy grip on the temptation to procrastinate.

Some interruptions fall into that procrastination trap quite well, so as we master procrastination we will, by default, limit some interruptions that accost our days. But other interruptions stop everything dead and demand immediate, complete attention. They rightfully require setting aside all other priorities and demands so we may address the source of the interruption. While in this chapter we'll consider some cures for the procrastination disease, in the next chapter we'll consider how to tell the difference between interruptions that warrant our attention and those that are part of the enemy's veiled plot to keep us from accomplishing God's purpose for our lives.

By observing my own tendencies and those of my staff members and colleagues, I have identified three primary culprits of procrastination: things I dread doing, things I don't know how to accomplish and things I don't think I can squeeze into my schedule. Let me show you how I've learned to push past these culprits.

Putting Things Off

I am a master at procrastination. You may be able to relate, being a master (or at least an aspiring master) at procrastination yourself. I put off projects that seem so overwhelming that I don't even know where to start or how to proceed if I do start them. But there are other tasks that I'm ashamed to admit I waste more time putting off than they'd take to accomplish. I procrastinate simply because I'm not looking forward to doing them. For example, I have surpassed amateur status at putting off low-priority or distasteful tasks like vacuuming (it makes my back ache), dusting (it makes me sneeze) and scraping gunk off the shower stall floor (it wreaks havoc on my fingernails). These are just a few of the tasks I don't mind admitting that I regularly procrastinate. Don't try to convince me that you don't do the same with these tasks and others like them—just about everyone has tasks that they'd rather do later or not at all.

> Procrastination is allowing things within our control to manipulate us into not doing what we know we ought to be doing.

In the greater scheme of things, whether I force myself to do these tasks once a week (as my grandmother does faithfully) or whether I get to them once a month, it probably doesn't matter much to too many people. However, other times the tasks I shrink from really do matter to other people. This morning was a perfect example. Since the most recent meeting of our single-adults group at church, I've had a list of new attendees to telephone and invite to our next get-together. For ten days I put off making the calls. I just couldn't bring myself to start them. Finally, this morning at 9 a.m., I stuffed the phone list into my purse. I was on my way out of town. My publicist was driving me to a nearby city for a radio interview. I had forty-five minutes before my cell phone and I left our home calling area. I made all ten calls with fifteen minutes to spare. Procrastinating had taken more time and energy than the actual calls.

We can blame interruptions for some of our lack of accomplishment, but sometimes it is our own wastefulness of precious moments that stands in the way of our successes.

I'd been waiting to free up a large block of time so I could socialize with everyone my calls caught at home, when all I needed was a purpose (waiting any longer would require long-distance charges) and thirty minutes that I'd otherwise have frittered away. During that half hour of calling, I spoke for a few moments with the one person I did catch at home (but didn't protract the conversation) and left messages for the rest.

We can blame interruptions for some of our lack of accomplishment, but sometimes it is our own wastefulness of precious moments that stands in the way of our successes. Which leads me back to the myth that serves as this chapter's title: give me a week without interruption, and I can really accomplish something. While we may think we need a week (or at least several hours) to accomplish a task, overestimates of the time we need may be putting us off starting a task that won't take so long after all.

Breaking Tasks Down

As we introduced the topic of procrastination, I admitted to you that there are some projects I put off simply because I don't know where to start—because they are too overwhelming for me to process, daunting to the very core. On these projects procrastination occurs when I adhere to the mistaken notion that to reach a goal I must find enough time to work through the task uninterrupted, proceeding from start to finish in one swoop. You know what I mean: Don't start reading that novel until you're sure you have enough time to read it from cover to cover. Don't start cleaning that closet until you can dump all of its contents in the center of the room and put them all back in their orderly places before dinner time. Don't start preparing that mailing until you have enough time to write the cover letter, run off the copies, print the address labels, stuff the envelopes and rush to the post office to mail them—all in one day.

As long as we buy into this "one-sitting fallacy" we'll never reach our goals.

If the assumption that we'll seldom find huge, uninterrupted blocks of time in most seasons of our lives is correct, then as long as we buy into this "one-sitting fallacy" we'll never reach our goals. Fortunately, I have good news: The one-sitting fallacy is just what its name indicates—a fallacy. It simply isn't true that we must have huge, uninterrupted blocks of time to reach our goals.

For big and potentially daunting projects, our first goal needs to be to create a doable plan of action—to establish an outline that lists the desired end result and a road map on how we intend to reach that end. In such a case, working backward from desired result to current starting point may be most efficient.

My client Jodi and her daughter Erin are a perfect example of this principle. Erin is a bright and vibrant teenager. She lives with her mother in a modest condo in the Midwest most of the year. She also spends blocks of time with her father in California. Over her nearly thirteen years Erin has collected more than her share of mementoes, reading material, clothes, toys, games and sundry discarded items from childhood. Every storage nook in her bedroom was filled with so many of these items that her current clothes, books and general "stuff" encroached on other areas of the condo.

Countless confrontations between mother and daughter ensued. Mother was angry that daughter's room was never tidy and that her "stuff" was cluttering shared areas of their home. Daughter thought mother was just picking on her.

Both agreed to talk with an impartial third party, who listened carefully and recognized that the source of the problem was not simply teenaged obstinacy—it was an accumulation of too much stuff. She proposed this solution: each day the two would spend as few as ten minutes sorting through the items in Erin's room. They'd make several piles: definite keepers; pass-along items to send to younger cousins and friends who might enjoy still-good clothes, games and books; long-term keepers that could be stored in an aunt's basement (a handy aunt to have); a couple of boxes to send to dad's apartment so it would feel like home during Erin's stays there; and items to toss.

It was a project that took several months to complete: one drawer, one shelf, one day at a time. However, when the project was completed, Erin's room was eminently more comfortable, one major conflict between mother and daughter was resolved and together they found a measure of joy in reminiscing about the times they'd spent together in years past playing the games, reading the books and choosing the clothes.

Scraps of Time

This project, undertaken by mother and daughter, demonstrates one of the most useful time management principles I have ever learned: when used wisely, scraps of time—even segments as small as five or ten minutes—can be the difference makers in achieving our goals. Jodi and Erin undertook their clean-up project in small chunks, one day at a time. In the end those few minutes per day allowed them to reach a substantial goal.

This principle of setting a large goal and accomplishing it in small chunks is credited to, of all people, good old Ben Franklin, according to Hyrum Smith, founder of the company that created the Franklin Day Planning System. Smith gave *Inc.* magazine an example of how this principle works: "If one of your governing values is to be financially independent, how will you attain that? . . . You must start a savings account, buy life insurance, and perhaps change careers. These little bites end up in your daily task lists."[1]

I liked the term "scraps of time" when I read it in a poem I encountered in a magazine years ago. While I've long since forgotten which magazine or who originally penned the phrase, it stuck in my mind nonetheless. It likely stuck because of my tendency to treat blocks of ten or twenty or thirty minutes tucked in between meetings as throw-away time, useless for any good purpose. My days are filled with scraps of time:

- Waiting for the buzzer to go off to check the cake I've just placed in the oven—after licking the bowl and washing the utensils, there's always at least thirty minutes to spare.

- Waiting for the family to finish getting ready to go to church—I always seem to be ready ten minutes ahead of the others.

- Waiting for my grandmother's doctor's appointment— her doctor always seems to run an hour behind schedule.

- Sitting on the commuter train in transit to and from a visit to a client—the only train I can get at my stop is a local, making all stops between my city and downtown Chicago.

We have two options in these times: we can tap a foot and check our watch and generally increase our level of frustration that others are causing us to waste precious time, or we can plan to come into those situations prepared with tasks that can be accomplished in those scraps of time. During the cake's baking, for example, I can call a sick friend who's been on my heart—in fact, now that I carry a cell phone in my purse, I can almost always use scraps of time to make phone calls. (I try not to do it, however, when I'm behind the wheel of the car.) Likewise, when I take one of my parents or my grandmother to the doctor's office, I now carry my laptop and writing notes with me, so I can work while I wait. (This sometimes leads to puzzled stares from elderly patients, whom I have more than once overheard making disparaging comments to each other in "stage whispers" on the affluence and fast-paced lives of people of my generation. Oh well, I guess it's another indication that we just can't please everyone.) And on the commuter train, I've begun reviewing notes I've taken in my meetings with clients or making one final refresher pass through the project I'm about to present.

Efficient use of scraps of time eliminates the increasing frustration I experience with others who are causing me to wait.

The benefits are twofold. First, projects move toward completion and items get checked off my to-do list. But even better for my own health and well-being, efficient use of scraps of time eliminates the increasing frustration I experience with others who are causing me to wait. My own blood pressure and digestive health improve as I wait more patiently.

Jesus and Scraps of Time

Even the time management principles of breaking tasks down into manageable bites and of making good use of each moment we receive from God's hand each day are rooted in good biblical soil.

Listen to the good counsel God gave to the Israelites through His servant Moses, recorded in Deuteronomy 11:18-21:

> Fix these words of mine in your hearts and minds; tie them as symbols on your hands and bind them on your foreheads. Teach them to your children, talking about them when you sit at home and when you walk along the road, when you lie down and when you get up. Write them on the doorframes of your houses and on your gates, so that your days and the days of your children may be many in the land that the LORD swore to give your forefathers, as many as the days that the heavens are above the earth.

The teachable moments of life, according to Moses' command and Jewish tradition, occur when you lie down and when you get up, when you sit at home and when you walk along the road. The Latin phrase *carpe diem* (seize the day) comes to mind. Seize the moments we might otherwise throw away to work toward achieving our goals, whether those goals entail passing along life principles to the next generation, finishing a project at work or painting the living room one roller stroke at a time.

When I look back at the notes I've made by observing the way Jesus spent His time during His earthly ministry, I also see glimmers of this principle. Jesus seldom had uninterrupted time with His followers and yet He somehow was able to communicate amazingly critical truths to them. How did He do it? I see Him seizing the moment as they walked together along the road, as they lay down to sleep for the night, as they ate their meals, sang their hymns and prayed their prayers.

Do we see Jesus doing a file dump of every gigabyte of data He ever wanted them to know in one sitting? Boom! Now you know everything there is to know about the kingdom of God. Not at all. Instead, we observe Jesus teaching His followers life lessons about His Father's kingdom in small doses. The kingdom of heaven is like a lost coin, a priceless pearl, a Father in search of His lost child. The kingdom of heaven is like a mustard seed, a little yeast, the wedding feast awaiting the bridegroom's coming. As He broke down the unsearchable riches of the kingdom of God into small, easy-to-understand bites, He also told His followers that He'd send Someone along behind Him (the Holy Spirit) to remind them of those things that were too difficult for them to process at that moment. The knowledge Jesus imparted to His followers accumulated into something great—and it was passed down to us in the New Testament. And yet, it was learned in countless short stories, memorable anecdotes, small revelations doled out one by one, making efficient use of each moment they spent with Him.

My Own Large Task

I have seen this learning method work in my life through a story I've since been able to share with many others. When I was under contract to write *Names of Women of the Bible*, I was employed full-time. My contract's stipulation was that the book must be completed in five months. That meant that after writing forty to fifty hours a week for my regular job, I had five months of evenings, holidays, vacations and weekends to write a book.

I had promised the publisher I'd profile fifty-two of the women in the Bible (so readers could study one a week for a year). This required fifty-two research trails, chapter outlines, first drafts, second drafts . . . you get the picture.

I counted out weeks and came up with this schedule: every Sunday I would research four women of the Bible. During the week, I would carry this research with me in my planner; whenever I had a few scraps of time (waiting for a meeting to start, sitting on an airplane, eating alone in a hotel restaurant, etc.) I'd work on the outlines. By the following Saturday, I would be ready to sit down and write the four chapters. This schedule would allow me to finish with two weeks to spare, in case unforeseen interruptions encroached on my well-laid schedule.

By Thanksgiving Day 1997, I'd reached my ambitious goal of writing an entire book in five months of evenings and weekends.

A Grandmother Uses Scraps of Time

As we conclude this discussion, let me share with you the story of my friend Leslie, who has just begun to pursue her life-long dream of training to become a professional writer. A few weeks into Leslie's pursuit of this dream, life sent her a road-block. Here's an excerpt from an e-mail she sent me last week:

> I'm faced with a test of my new priorities—my grand-daughter just entered kindergarten and needs to be picked up and taken care of after school every day. She only attends for half a day. Daycare would be a good solution, but the money isn't there for that. . . . My specific question then is how to stay on course with my goals while not abandoning my responsibilities. I am not sure if there is a practical solution. I've been praying for guidance and help with the

frustration that I'm feeling. Any ideas would be greatly appreciated.

My main suggestion to Leslie was that she follow the same principle that I had discovered during my writing of *Names of Women of the Bible*. I wrote back to her and said:

> The good news is that bits and pieces of time (I call them scraps), if used effectively, can be just as productive as big chunks of time. Do you wait in the car for ten minutes before your granddaughter comes out of school? Maybe you can use that time to read a portion of your lesson or to jot down some thoughts in answer to a question. Or maybe you can do something that's more mundane—jot down a shopping list or use your cell phone to make a call you've not had time to make. . . . You may be surprised at how many throwaway minutes we each waste in a day.
>
> Does your granddaughter like to color, draw, practice her letters and numbers, read or watch videos? If so, you might set up your computer on a table in the room where she is. Then, you can practice your work while she does her "work." Does your granddaughter like the library? You might find out whether your public library has story time for kids—if so, she can be entertained there and you can use the library's quiet room (or reference room or Internet-equipped computers) for some work time. She'll be having fun and you'll be productive as well.

I sent these ideas and a few more to Leslie the day I received her e-mail. Within a few hours she had zapped this response to me:

> Julie, this is great advice. After writing you this morning, I talked to the Lord about it again and felt like He was leading me to do basically what you suggested about bits and

snatches of time. I did, and it actually worked! I was amazed at how much I was able to accomplish. I also was able to enjoy the time my granddaughter and I spent together. It was encouraging to get your e-mail this afternoon, saying the same thing I had been impressed with this morning and getting more information about how to do it more effectively. Thank you so much! I have hope again.

Challenge of the Week

As you prepare to read the next chapter, which delves further into the subject of interruptions, review what we know about the life of Christ as recorded by Matthew, Mark, Luke and John. See if you can find some of the interruptions Jesus and His followers encountered. Record any questions you would like to ask Him about how He chose to handle them.

Endnote

1. "The Custom-Made Day Planner" [on-line], February 1, 1992. *Inc.* magazine. September 16, 2002. Available from: <http://www.inc.com/magazine/19920201/3920.html>.

Myth: I must always make time for every
interruption that comes across my path.

In the last chapter, we discussed the concept of breaking
tasks down into manageable bites to keep the everyday,
garden-variety interruption of procrastination from overwhelming us and keeping us from our goals. In this chapter,
we'll take a closer look at another aspect of taking charge of interruptions: recognizing their source and controlling those interruptions that are controllable.

I am thinking of some interruptions that have taken place
during my writing of this book. Illnesses of myself and my
loved ones would count, as would time-sensitive projects that
have come in unexpectedly from long-time and new clients, and
a long-awaited office/home move right as I was preparing to
commit this chapter to disk.

But the biggest interruption is one far outside my control. In
fact, it is one that began to impact your life on the same day as it
impacted mine. Here is an entry from my journal:

> Today is September 11, 2001; already it is being described as a
> day that will live in infamy. I had been planning to research
> the chapter on interruptions today. How pathetically timely.
>
> As I write, the entire nation has experienced a complete in-
> terruption, a lock-down situation precipitated by the terror-
> ist events that took place on the campus of the World Trade
> Center, the Pentagon and a field in Pennsylvania.
>
> Tens of thousands of lives have been interrupted today.
> We don't yet know how many lives have been snuffed out;

but it is sure to be thousands. Yet these are not the only ones interrupted: I see business-suit clad New Yorkers covered with soot, traversing bridges by foot in a frantic scramble to safety; medical personnel staying on duty for shift upon shift with no let up in sight; security and rescue personnel called to sacrifice their personal safety at the scenes. To say nothing of stunned financial markets, grounded airplanes and everyday people clustered around TVs and radios in their homes or offices.

Every life has been interrupted. My cousin's two-year-old daughter is left indefinitely in the care of her nanny, as her parents, both commercial pilots, are diverted to Newfoundland. She wants her mommy. She is inconsolable.

As I stare at my TV screen, I am watching at least one textbook example of handling interruptions: every broadcast TV station in the country has preempted all programming—including advertisements—to provide continuous commentary, video and analysis of the events. Under normal circumstances not even one commercial would be preempted on any network during the broadcast day. The networks' survival in everyday times depends upon the finances generated by ads. However, these are not everyday times, and the network executives have determined to heed this necessary interruption by throwing 100 percent of their resources into the dissemination of good, timely and complete information to the dazed and furious American public.

It is, after all, their first goal as the fourth estate, to facilitate and disseminate unbiased and uncensored news to the public; this I learned back in journalism school. But never have I seen it so poignantly played out before my eyes. Today the media's companion goal of financial viability has been superceded by the higher goal of providing information. I'd definitely call that an interruption.

This scenario describes by example how we make timely, informed choices when goals compete with each other. It reaffirms the necessity of setting and prioritizing our goals *before* we encounter situations where they will conflict. And it is an eloquent example of handling interruptions based upon those choices.

How this concept translates to those of us who, as believers in Christ, daily face competing choices is the next subject we'll consider.

Schedule for the Unforeseen

I had just celebrated reaching the halfway point of writing my first book when I reached a writing plateau. I've never liked the term "writer's block," but it got a hold of me nonetheless. I was caught up on my researching and chapter outlining, and I sat down at my desk that Saturday morning thinking I was ready to write: coffee cup full, to my right; notes reviewed and assembled, to my left; Mozart providing background from the CD player behind my desk. I prayed and then opened the computer file. And nothing.

I'd been through a particularly rough week and was already having trouble focusing my mind. Then, although I wasn't answering it myself, I kept hearing the phone ringing and ringing. The distraction was more than I could handle.

It didn't take more than thirty minutes of staring at a blank screen and listening to the incessant clanging of the phone before I began to feel the pressure levels increasing. According to my schedule, I needed to write 4,000 words that day. But, despite the knowledge of that goal hanging over my head, I could scarcely put together a sentence. After four hours I'd only achieved 1,000 words. Normally, I'd write until I was finished with the 4,000 words, whether it took six hours or twelve. That day, though, I gave up, stopped writing and stalked away from the computer.

After I'd gained some perspective I realized that while I was entitled to be disappointed, I need not escalate to the panic stage because, as I mentioned in the previous chapter, I've learned to expect the unexpected. I'd set my writing schedule to accommodate two writing days that didn't go well—or at all. So, this interruption was all part of the plan. Instead of obsessing about the writer's block, I went for a long walk and then drove to the Saturday night service at my church.

We can alleviate panic if we schedule a time cushion for ourselves whenever possible.

Whether it's a phone call from a friend who is in tears and needs someone to just listen and understand, an unscheduled bout of writer's block or a national catastrophe, our well-planned schedules are going to be interrupted by things beyond our control. But we can alleviate panic if we schedule a time cushion for ourselves whenever possible. If an article is due January 15, I make plans to finish it by January 8; then if my Internet connection goes down for a day or so, I don't have to pay to send the manuscript next day air. If a book is due November 30, I try to finish the first draft by November 1, let it sit for at least a week, then read and edit it a final time, finishing this process a week before my publisher expects to receive it.

Likewise, I counsel my college writing students that it's really not a good idea to start writing their term papers or studying for their final exam at midnight when it's due at 8 o'clock the next morning. You never know when the electricity is going to go out in the dorm, or the roommate is going to turn on her stereo full blast and paint her nails at 2 a.m. or the student council is going to order midnight pizza for everyone who'll come to the commons.

Expect the unexpected. This is one way to exercise control over otherwise uncontrollable circumstances.

Control What You Can

While it has become clichéd, the anonymous Serenity Prayer has made its numerous appearances on plaques and friendship cards for one simple reason: it rings true. "Lord, grant me the serenity to accept the things I cannot change, the ability to change the things I can and the wisdom to know the difference."

This reminds us that there are some things we can control. Just as we can control procrastination with good planning and level-headed consideration of our options, so too can we control many of the interruptions that accost us.

In my single adults group at church we've recently completed a multi-month series on setting boundaries. While some of the sessions centered around boundaries in dating, others got into boundaries in families and with friends and even in the workplace. These are difficult to set, we concluded, but necessary if we are to maintain our individual sanity. Firm, well-established boundaries are exactly what we need to control interruptions.

For example, back in the olden days, we only received mail once a day. Now our days are interrupted by four kinds of mail: express mail, e-mail, voice mail and snail-mail. Our days have never before been so replete with mail-related interruptions. When I worked at Moody Bible Institute, my computer was directly wired into the network and my e-mail icon flashed every time I received a new item in my box—from the Institute's intranet, as well as from the outside world (Internet). I am curious by nature, but I learned to set boundaries that limited the number of times I'd check my e-box. I settled on three times a day: upon arriving in the morning, upon returning from lunch and once more a half hour before leaving for the day. The same went for my voice mail box. Without this discipline, I'd bounce aimlessly from interruption to interruption without making any progress on my to-do list and my frustration needle would reach the critical level before lunchtime every day.

Likewise, I learned to set space boundaries by closing my door (when my office had a door) or tying a flag across the entrance to my cubicle that said something like: "Genius at work, enter at your own risk." This not only provided a chuckle to passersby, but more importantly it limited gratuitous conversation (and let my boss know I was serious about meeting his deadlines).

Now that I work out of my home, I've learned to set boundaries that let my family know when I'm under the deadline crunch. Of course, these boundaries go both ways: I respect their space when they need it, and they respect mine. I've even been known to set boundaries by letting the answering machine screen my calls—thus eliminating interruptions from telephone sales reps trying to sell me new windows or a new roof when I don't even own my own home. I'll then return necessary calls all at one time, taking one interruption rather than a series of annoying ones. This means I only have to restart my work once and I am less likely to have to stop writing mid-sentence—which is particularly unpleasant.

I learned the boundaries lesson back when I lived in a college dorm. The temptation was to say yes every time someone would pass by my door announcing, "We're ordering pizza; wanna join us?" I quickly learned that if I were to keep my grades up (necessary to keep my academic scholarship), I couldn't be indiscriminate in following my nose to every room that reeked of soggy cardboard pizza boxes. I learned to hold my responses until I could ask and answer these internal questions, *Am I far enough ahead in my studies to warrant a one- or two-hour interruption for pizza and chat time? Can I or can I not afford the time tonight?* It came down to choices and priorities.

Jesus Makes the Call

Whole books have been written on making choices, and far be it for me to prescribe the way you must make your choices. I make mine, for better or worse, after much thought, much prayer and much discussion with trusted advisors. I tend not to be spontaneous, but rather deliberate in my decision-making processes.

> Jesus demonstrates that it is possible to make the difficult calls in life: to please God, even when disappointing beloved humans.

Whether you are deliberate or spontaneous, you can be comforted, as I am, by the Bible passage we read in chapter 1 that says of Jesus, "For we do not have a high priest who is unable to sympathize with our weaknesses, but we have one who has been tempted in every way, just as we are—yet was without sin" (Hebrews 4:15). This comforts—and challenges—me because Jesus demonstrates that it is possible to make the difficult calls in life: to please God, even when disappointing beloved humans. He was faced with the same tests and temptations we see daily yet He faced and conquered them in the strength His Father provided to Him and also offers to us.

How did Christ handle interruptions? In answer, I ask you to notice the juxtaposition of two storylines in Mark 5:21-42. Verses 21 and 22 introduce us to Jairus, the important, wealthy synagogue ruler who begs Jesus for the favor of healing his only child. It seems to me that if Jesus does this favor for the important ruler, He'll be ingratiated to the entire synagogue congregation—not a bad group to have on His side. So I am not surprised when verse 24 announces, "So Jesus went with him." *Way to go, Jesus. Now you're playing the power game.*

But what happens next amazes me. There is a huge crowd pressing in on Jesus and his entourage. Suddenly Jesus stops and asks this profound question, "Who touched me?" Jairus and the disciples must have been at least as amazed as I. "What do you mean? Don't you see the crowd? *Everybody* touched you. C'mon, if You're going to do the little girl any good You've got to hurry." (That is the Julie translation, but it is a fairly accurate depiction, according to scriptural accounts.)

Jesus is unthwarted. "I felt power go out from me," He says. So He stays put, keeps waiting, keeps scanning the crowd, until a woman throws herself at His feet and blurts out her story: She had been subject to hemorrhaging for twelve years, had spent all her money on doctors and remedies and had not received one moment's respite. So, she determined to touch Jesus' robe in the belief that if she were successful she'd be healed. Sure enough, the moment she touched His robe, the bleeding stopped.

Jesus allowed her to be healed at the moment she reached for His robe, but He didn't allow her to escape into the crowd unnoticed. Instead, He took this God-ordained interruption to restore the woman's wounded spirit, and in so doing to teach us a lesson in handling our own interruptions. He looked her in the eye and called her "daughter." He commended her faith. He validated her. He healed her spirit as well as her body.

An interesting side note: This interruption seems to cost a little girl her life as Jairus' daughter dies. But at the end of the story, Jesus raises the girl and returns her to her parents.

Through these juxtaposed stories, Jesus teaches us to value individual souls, to be sensitive to His Spirit's quiet nudges, to wait expectantly for as long as it takes for a wounded heart to pour out its woes and then to apply soothing salve over long-carried wounds. He shows us how to do all this even when the ensuing interruptions throw off our already crowded agendas.

Unscrambling Competing Goals

So, then, are we to embrace indiscriminately every interruption that comes our way? Surely not. Let's turn to Jesus again:

> Jesus began to explain to his disciples that he must go to Jerusalem and suffer many things at the hands of the elders, chief priests and teachers of the law, and that he must be killed and on the third day be raised to life.
>
> Peter took him aside and began to rebuke him. "Never, Lord!" he said. "This shall never happen to you!"
>
> Jesus turned and said to Peter, "Get behind me, Satan! You are a stumbling block to me; you do not have in mind the things of God, but the things of men." (Matthew 16:21-23)

Jesus, who is usually kind and tender and patient with His sometimes-slow-to-understand followers, spends some pretty harsh words on Peter: "Get behind me, Satan!" If it were a cartoon, it would be punctuated with a "Pow!" Maybe even with a double exclamation point!! Peter thinks he is being savvy and protective of his Master. He thinks he's doing right in interrupting Jesus. Yet Jesus says, "You're trying to interrupt My Father's plan. I won't let you do that. Your interruption is not of God, but of the enemy. I will not allow you to stand in My way."

Discerning the Source

Many times in Jesus' life He allowed Himself to be interrupted by genuine seekers of truth, by people who needed His touch or by bruised and battered hearts perishing alone. But at other times, such as in this scene with Peter, Jesus set His face like flint and would allow nothing to deter Him.

How did He know the difference? And how can we recognize the difference in our own lives? It is a matter of discernment, a matter of knowing God's will so confidently that there is no question as to the source of the interruption in our path.

As we proceed through this study, we'll talk more about the ways we can learn to discern God's voice clearly, but for now let me just say that it requires our silence before Him; it calls for focused study of His Word and persistence in voicing our prayers and waiting attentively for His answers. I love the passage in Isaiah's prophecy where God promises His faithful ones, "Whether you turn to the right or to the left, your ears will hear a voice behind you, saying, 'This is the way; walk in it' " (Isaiah 30:21). As we gain more and more practice in listening for this gentle voice, we'll be better able to discern for ourselves whether, when interruptions tempt us to turn to the right or the left, we hear the voice of God's Spirit directing us to take the interruption or to treat it as a roadblock keeping us from accomplishing His purposes.[1]

Challenge of the Week

There is one interruption I look to with anticipation and expectancy: the one that will occur when Jesus returns, when graves open and we who are alive are taken up to be with Him forever. It is the hope of that day that keeps me focused, on-track and intentional about how I spend each moment of the day I'm living today. If you too are looking forward to that day, search the Scriptures for references to the rapture and to what our timeless, forever home will be like. Begin with these: First Corinthians 15:50-52, First Thessalonians 4:14-5:11 and Revelation 22:1-17.

Endnote

1. For a detailed study of this subject, pick up a copy of my book, *Praying Like Jesus* (Moody Press, 2001).

Myth: I'm expected to be completely self-motivated, self-sufficient and self-directed.

When I was a young manager making my first hiring decision, I sought out counsel from a variety of sources on the kind of person to consider for the job I was trying to fill. I was well aware of the detailed qualifications listed on the job description, and of course I wouldn't consider someone for the position who didn't have the technical skills and training required to perform those tasks. But choosing one from among a list of equally qualified candidates seemed to me to require something akin to the wisdom of Solomon.

I thought back to my own job interviews, and I considered the high marks and nods of acknowledgment I always seemed to receive when I admitted to being a self-starter or an internally driven Type-A person who works well with minimal oversight. And yet a smattering of interviewers asked whether I felt I could be a team player (could I put the company's goals ahead of my own personal goals? could I pinch hit for my colleagues without seeking recognition for myself?). Different interviewers, it seemed, were looking for wholly different types of people. Which kind of person was right for this job? I didn't have a clue.

So, I read books. I asked questions of our human resources managers. I listened to my colleagues' anecdotes about good and bad hiring decisions—I needed only to look down the line of cubicles outside my office to see examples of both the good and the bad. Some sources suggested I look for a self-started, self-motivated, independent thinker who would need little more direction than a vision statement and job description. Others suggested I look for a team player who would prize loyalty and meeting department goals ahead of personal achievement.

It all left me rather dizzy, as advisors contradicted each other and offered little precise assistance in my decision making. Ultimately, the decision was mine. I was feeling very much alone. And in my aloneness, I was spending more time and energy obsessing about the decision than I could afford. So much for being a self-starting, internally driven, Type-A person.

Before I let you in on the choice I eventually made, I'd like for us to examine several issues this scenario raises, with the goal of isolating and solving the problems inherent when we approach our time usage as if we were utterly self-contained and self-sufficient.

Acknowledging that I Needed Help

In my quest for counsel, I did right and I did wrong. But before we dissect the downside of the advice I received, let's look first at the upside of my search. I was correct in acknowledging that I was ill-equipped to face the task on my own with no need for outside assistance.

Such is the case with nearly every task in life. The writer of Ecclesiastes was apparently a man of inherent wisdom; yet he acknowledged,

> Two are better than one,
>   because they have a good return for their work:
> If one falls down,
>   his friend can help him up.

But pity the man who falls
   and has no one to help him up!
Also, if two lie down together,
   they will keep warm.
But how can one keep warm alone?
Though one may be overpowered,
   two can defend themselves.
A cord of three strands is not quickly broken.

(Ecclesiastes 4:9-12)

God, in His infinite wisdom, did not create us for a life of solitariness. He created us for community, for togetherness, for companionship. In sinning, our forbearers condemned us to a tenuous kind of community—one that resembles more a tug of war (us against them) mentality than the Creator's original plan of companionable unity. Nevertheless, we yearn for each other; we need each other; we see life as frightening, overwhelming, even excruciating when we are left alone for too long.

> God, in His infinite wisdom, did not create us for a life of solitariness. He created us for community, for togetherness, for companionship.

Even in our penal system the ultimate in punishment is to constrain an inmate to a term of *solitary* confinement. And yet many of us so prize our independence that we refuse to ask for help when we need it, for a listening ear when our own voices are echoing against hollow walls, for a strong arm to support us when we're faltering. The *Holman Bible Handbook* explains it this way: "Christian living is meant to be a shared experience. . . . [It assumes] mutual encouragement, enlightenment, accountability, and discipline."[1]

The Big Accountability Dilemma

One of the most helpful ways we can acknowledge this need for support and trusted relationships as we seek to use our time resources wisely is in the concept of accountability, a subject the *Holman* quote mentions in passing. In this supportive sort of accountability I not only acknowledge responsibility for my choices, but willingly submit to the scrutiny of another person (a trusted person, to be sure).

Lest this sound disagreeable to our liberty-indoctrinated, twenty-first-century minds, let me tell you a story that demonstrates the payback accountability can have in our scheduling.

I consider myself, for better or worse, a professional writer. It's my career, one for which I've trained, one I've practiced for years, one that keeps a roof over my head and my tummy fed. I'm not bad at what I do; I've had some measure of critical and marketing success. Nevertheless, while I love *having written*, the process of actually committing words to a computer screen is often a painful and difficult one. When it comes time to write, I am tempted to do all manner of other tasks. I'll suddenly develop an interest in, say, dusting or vacuuming (you already know how I feel about those tasks), in surfing the web (I call it research, but we both know otherwise) or in doing just about anything but writing.

Knowing this about myself, I recognize that this is one trait I need help to conquer. So, I've asked my assistant to participate in the process. I let her in on the writing goals I've established (such as the need to commit a certain number of publishable words to disk every writing day), and then gave her permission to hold me accountable to meeting those goals.

When I'm at my computer, supposedly writing, I'll hear her padding down the hall. Sometimes she comes bearing an always-welcome pot of steaming coffee. Now, if I am indeed found to be on task, doing my writing, she'll deposit the coffee and back away silently. If, however, I'm found doing anything but writing, she'll sit in my guest chair for a moment or two and then say gently, "Don't you think it's time you got back to work on that chapter?"

The key to accountability happens right at that moment. If I snap back with a snotty remark about it being my prerogative to spend my time however I wish, she'll not come in to keep me on task tomorrow. However, if I grin and say, "You're right; I'll get back to it," she'll continue her part of the bargain—she'll keep on holding me to the schedule I've set. Since I know she'll be checking on me (unannounced), I'm more likely to stay on task to begin with—rather than bear the disapproving glance when I've wandered from the path. That's what accountability can do for me.

I told this story to a conference audience not long ago. In the audience was a fellow author, a successful novelist who has the same love/hate relationship with the writing process as I have. Unbeknownst to me, she'd been struggling with meeting a deadline for months. After hearing my story, she decided to give her husband permission to hold her accountable. A month after I returned home, I received an e-mail from her thanking me for sharing my story, and letting me know it worked for her, helping her stay on task until she met her deadline. She told me that she came away with the added benefit of her husband feeling like a valued member of the writing team—not doing the writing, but "holding up the arms" of the one who was (see Exodus 17:10-13).

When It's Good to Be Alone

Now, before we get too excited about community and accountability and Solomon's advice that "Plans go wrong for lack of advice; many counselors bring success" (Proverbs 15:22, NLT), let me tell you that many counselors may also bring contradiction. The story about my hiring decision is tribute to this fact: Every individual on a team, within an organization, even within the church family will have his own opinion. Every opinion holder will believe his is the only right way. And nearly every opinion will be proven both right and wrong. Or, more specifically, partially right and partially wrong.

The time will come, after we have sought out counsel from the best and wisest, when we'll just have to get alone with God to seek direction. As we touched upon in the previous chapter, we often read in the Gospels about Jesus going alone to pray, to seek the counsel, communion and relationship of His heavenly Father.

> ## The time will come, after we have sought out counsel from the best and wisest, when we'll just have to get alone with God to seek direction.

I am intrigued that Jesus' biggest staffing decision—His choice of twelve close associates in ministry—came immediately after a time of aloneness with His Father. Luke describes the setting this way:

> One of those days Jesus went out to a mountainside to pray, and spent the night praying to God. When morning came, he called his disciples to him and chose twelve of them, whom he also designated apostles. (Luke 6:12-13)

If such decisions drove the Son of God to seek His Father's guidance in an overnight prayer session, how much more ought they drive me to spend precious moments, hours, even days in prayer over the decisions that affect my life and the lives of my employees, family or friends? Is it time consuming? Yes. Is it a time expenditure we can afford to cut out of our busy schedules? Certainly not!

There came a point—after I had sorted through all of the human counsel—that I needed to carry my options, choices, concerns and opportunities to God. My purpose was not to receive His stamp of approval on a choice I'd already made, but rather to lay it all out before Him and await the direction of His calm, quiet voice.

Are We Alone When We Feel Alone?

I remember a line that I heard on a TV drama several years ago; I remember it because its desperation has haunted me ever since. The lead character had a decision to make. Her best friend had, earlier in the program, pledged his lifelong support of her cause. In the course of the hour's events, however, he vehemently disagreed with a key decision she made that affected both of them. He disagreed so vehemently that he stalked out of her office in fury. It was at this point that she whispered in the hearing of no one other than herself, "I guess I really am alone after all."

> The good news is that we need not place our full faith and trust in mere mortals.

It is tragic to realize that someone we've come to count on would choose to walk away when we need him the most, but unfortunately that's the way people can be sometimes. The good news is, however, that we need not place our full faith and trust in mere mortals. Rather, we can place our trust in the immutable God who makes the following promises and has kept His word for time immemorial:

- I will not leave you comfortless (John 14:18, KJV).
- I am in you (John 14:20).
- I will never leave you nor forsake you (Hebrews 13:5, NKJV).

So, even when we—as followers of Jesus—feel alone, we can have the real-life assurance that we are never truly alone. How can I be so convinced? Again, look at Jesus' ministry. He worked side-by-side with His followers on Earth, providing them with all of the resources they needed to accomplish the tasks to which He called them. He also sent behind Him the rich counsel of the Holy Spirit to continue to guide and provide for them in His absence.

It is interesting to note that when Jesus sent His disciples out to minister, He sent them not one by one, but two by two (Mark 6:7). (We're back to the companionship thing again.) More importantly, though, notice that He gave them the power and authority of His name to use as they encountered good and bad situations. He gives us that same authority, and we live under the same promises that our predecessors have enjoyed for more than 2,000 years.

So ultimately, was the hiring decision truly mine? In my power-hungry humanness I'd like to have thought so, but it wasn't. God was with me, as He promised He'd be. And although I felt alone when it came time to make that final choice, I was actually in the best company I'd ever shared, because God was beside me all the way.

The Risk of Extremes

One of the major reasons I had so much difficulty in making that hiring decision was because I had received so much counsel from so many well-meaning sources. The extremes of their advice put them at opposite ends of the hiring spectrum. I saw some truth in each side's opinions, but neither seemed sufficient to apply to my particular situation. Could there be some creative solution that would incorporate all of these truths?

After some consideration, I realized scriptural accounts of Jesus' life were relevant even to my hiring dilemma. Finding the middle ground, the creative solution, was an area in which Jesus excelled—to the great frustration of the nosy Pharisees. Consider the time when Jesus found Himself trapped between condemning the adulterous woman or condoning her sin. In this case, He located and chose the middle path of hating the sin but loving the sinner. Here's how the scene is introduced in John chapter 8:

> The teachers of the law and the Pharisees brought in a woman caught in adultery. They made her stand before the group and said to Jesus, "Teacher, this woman was caught in the act of adultery. In the Law Moses commanded us to stone such women. Now what do you say?" They were using this question as a trap, in order to have a basis for accusing him.
>
> But Jesus bent down and started to write on the ground with his finger. When they kept on questioning him, he straightened up and said to them, "If any one of you is without sin, let him be the first to throw a stone at her." (John 8:3-7)

Well, then, you meddling Pharisees, take that!

Since our Lord is a master of creative solutions to complex dilemmas, I had yet another reason (as if I needed more) to carry this choice to Him in prayer. After much prayer, I realized my creative solution required hiring a staff person who wouldn't operate in a vacuum, but also wouldn't need me to hold his hand or direct every task. After studying the resumes I'd read and the interview notes I'd taken, I found just the person. She seemed most teachable, most adaptable and most ready to pitch in with the group when it was required, but also most able to work independently under everyday circumstances. I offered her the job and she accepted.

My choice turned out to be a good one, as the individual I hired was later promoted by one of my colleagues, became one of my first clients when I started my own business and continues to be someone I call friend. Now that wasn't so hard, after all.

Challenge of the Week

Read the story of the Israelites as they battled an ancient foe in Exodus 17:8-13. Note especially the unique method of participation Aaron and Hur had in the battle. Record your thoughts here.

Then consider who among your colleagues, family or friends might be a candidate for keeping you accountable, holding up your arms, helping you work toward your goals. Then, go to that person and propose a reciprocal relationship: "I'll hold you accountable, if you'll hold me accountable."

Endnote

1. David S. Dockery, ed., *Holman Bible Handbook* (Nashville, TN: Holman Bible Publishers, 1992), p. 845.

Myth: I'm responsible to meet every need of everyone
at every time in every venue of my life.

Closely related to the Lone Ranger complex we discussed in the previous chapter is the myth that we can
do and be everything everyone in our lives needs at every moment of every day. That's a tall order. And since there is one
God and we are not He, it's one we can't fulfill. When we make
our futile attempts to do the work that is actually set aside for
someone else to accomplish, we shirk our own responsibilities,
misuse our own time resources and build our frustration (or
even anger) levels to fuse-blowing proportions.

It can be a subtle temptation, this self-importance complex.
Consider the scene of a mom in the kitchen with her child. The
child wants to bake a batch of cookies. She is hardly tall enough to
see over the counter, so she must stand on a chair to mix the ingredients. As youngsters will be, the child is rather clumsy when she
pours ingredients into the mixing bowl. Before long, there is egg
and milk and unidentified sticky gook splattered on counter, floor
and little girl's blouse. When flour goes into the bowl, well, suffice
it to say that few fixtures in the room are spared from the snowy
white billows of powder dust. The chocolate chips fare no better.
The bag spills across the counter and the little girl is caught gig-
gling, with a fistful of chips on their way into her mouth.

The mother has a critical choice to make. Clearly, it would be
easier for her to make the cookies herself. The little girl would en-

67

joy eating them and the mother wouldn't have a head-to-toe mess
to clean up. Yet, the mother knows her daughter will not earn her
cooking badge in her club troop if she doesn't do the entire process herself. She also knows that if her daughter isn't allowed to
make the mistakes necessary to learn to mix a bowl of cookie
dough, she will never progress to the next level in her kitchen education. And, she realizes that although standing back will take all
of her self-discipline to accomplish, it is the right thing to do. So,
rather than taking the wooden mixing spoon from the little girl's
hand and banishing her to the twelfth showing of a Barney movie
on the video player, the mom smiles and watches her little girl
awkwardly come to terms with a new skill, thinking back on similar scenes in her own life when her mother let her make her own
mistakes—in the kitchen and in the outside world.

One of the greatest drains on our time is when we attempt to do other people's work.

This example, while seemingly trivial, illustrates a powerful
concept. Even when we are in a position of authority (at home
or at work), we must allow those for whom we are responsible
to do their work in their own way (even if we think we could do
a better job ourselves).

The Virtues of Delegating

One of the greatest drains on our time is when we attempt to
do other people's work, whether it is because we feel we're the
only ones who can, because we feel we can do it better ourselves, because we're too distracted to show them how or because we're afraid to trust them to complete the task. Indeed we
may be responsible to show them how, but then we need to get
out of the way and let them find the best way to accomplish the
task.

Maybe it's just a woman thing, but I always think I have identified the only and best way to accomplish a task. Whether it's mixing cookie dough in the kitchen, cleaning the bathtub or writing an article, I always seem to like my way best. When it comes time to equip someone else to work on a task, I am tempted to force them into doing it the same way I do it, the "right" way. Except, the way that is right to my sensibilities, my unique physiology and my mind-set may be awkward or unattainable to the delegatee. Instead, that person may just find a better, more efficient or at least more comfortable way for him to accomplish a task.

It is my responsibility to communicate the vision, goal or desired outcome. It is my responsibility to equip that person with the tools necessary to accomplish the proper outcome. Then it is my responsibility to back off and trust him to do the work. (I can be available to answer questions from a distance, but I ought not stand over his shoulder to watch every mistake or divergent choice he may make along the way.)

For example, say we are putting together a mailing in our office. My way would be to print out piles containing just enough of each piece of the mailing (stuffing items, cover letters, mailing labels, etc.), spread out each of the piles across the table, fold the items together, sticker each envelope, place the items in the envelopes, stamp and seal them all at once and drive off to the post office to mail them immediately. However, when I delegate the task to my volunteer assistant Joy, I need to allow her to find her own best way to stuff the mailing. She may sticker the envelopes first or fold the items in a different way or print the mailing from the computer in collated order (to save the assembly step). And, as much as I'd like to be right, Joy just might find a more efficient or effective way of achieving the same goal. I just need to get out of the way and let her work.

The Limitations of Humanness

Consider this powerful reminder of the way Jesus chose to conduct Himself on this planet:

> Your attitude should be the same that Christ Jesus had. Though he was God, he did not demand and cling to his rights as God. He made himself nothing; he took the humble position of a slave and appeared in human form. And in human form he obediently humbled himself even further by dying a criminal's death on a cross. (Philippians 2:5-8, NLT)

What a comfort to know that there is Someone who can willingly meet the deepest needs of every one of us, and every one of those people we care for and love.

This Scripture passage both comforts and haunts me. Jesus, by setting aside his rights and privileges as God, willingly limited Himself to the created elements of time and space. These constraints allowed Him to be in but one place at one time, just as you and I are so constrained. This is one of the reasons He told His disciples it was good if He returned to Heaven and sent His Spirit to be in them in His place: "But I tell you the truth: It is for your good that I am going away. Unless I go away, the Counselor will not come to you; but if I go, I will send him to you" (John 16:7). The Holy Spirit was to be unencumbered by the human limitations of time and space. He would be omnipresent—present everywhere at every time. This is beyond our limited understanding, yet it is nonetheless comforting to know. He is truly everything to us, meeting every need of every believer at every moment.

What a comfort to know that there is Someone who can willingly meet the deepest needs of every one of us, and every one of those people we care for and love. The challenging part is when I come face-to-face with the fact that I cannot fill that role. When I try to, I run smack against the wall of my human limitations. I become irritable, overstretched, taxed beyond my limits. And at those moments, my attitude is the farthest possible from the one Jesus modeled, which was one of humility, of servanthood, of self-sacrifice, rather than self-importance.

I can recall vividly many scenes in my life when this limitation became eminently clear. Many of these scenes revolve around teaching colleagues, students or staff members to use computers. For better or worse, I tend to be rather intuitive about operating computer software. If one method doesn't work, I'll instinctively know another method to try. I'm driven to find a solution that will work. And I usually do find it. Don't ask me how—I just do. I couldn't tell you how I know what else to try. I just "fiddle" around with the keyboard and mouse, and somehow I get the desired result on the screen.

This is great in my own business, because I seldom need to incur the expense of consulting with a computer technician. However, when I'm training someone else in computer use and he runs across a problem, that's when my I'll-just-do-it-myself-because-it's-easier-than-showing-you-how mechanism kicks into gear. This fosters the staffer's dependence upon me, which I secretly rather enjoy. I feel important, knowledgeable and a little more powerful if he can't do his job without asking me to sit down at his computer and make it do what he needs it to do.

But what happens to that staffer when I'm not around? when I'm in a meeting? when I'm on a cruise or at a convention or out of town or home sick? My self-importance has kept him ignorant of the workings of his computer and unable to function without me by his side. This is not a healthy method of operation, as any trainer or leader will know.

I can't always be there for him—remember those human limitations? Instead, I need to be a good enough trainer to equip
my employee to do the work himself, much like that mom who
allows her daughter to mix the cookie dough herself. Every
good leader knows that delegating tasks to the up-and-comers
is good management. Why? I had one boss who explained that
he already was grooming someone to take his place. His reason
was, "If I get hit by a bus when I'm stepping off the curb tonight, I know who I'd want to keep the work going—and he's
already equipped to make an almost seamless transition."

Bringing junior leaders along is good management, but it is
also risky. We need to be secure enough in our positions and
self-worth not to be looking over our shoulders, jealous of others catching up behind us.

Regardless of the risks, though, these time management dilemmas remind me to beware of the danger of trying to take God's
place in people's lives. He and only He can meet the needs of every individual. It is my own pride and self-importance that, if un-
checked, can get in the way of God accomplishing His purposes in
the lives of my colleagues and friends, as well as in my own life.

Clearing My Schedule

The other benefit of delegating tasks we can "spin off" of our
own agendas is that we can be more focused on the tasks we are
uniquely qualified to take on.

In the kind of work that I do, clients pay for my specific exper-
tise, my experience, my talents and my abilities. The actual writing
and speaking and public relations tasks I am paid to perform, I
must undertake myself. However, there are other tangentially related tasks I can delegate to Joy. She can screen phone calls (most
of them she can handle without my oversight); she can make the
last proofreading pass through my finished manuscripts; she can

handle booking my speaking engagements (including negotiating fees, obtaining travel instructions, booking transportation, etc.); she can make some of the promotional sales calls needed to obtain new clients.

I've given her good parameters in each of these areas, she is skilled and well-trained and she knows from experience how much she can do without my intervention. Joy feels valued (she is invaluable to me, and I express that to her often) and I feel less stress about having to handle the aspects of my business that someone else can shoulder for me.

This is delegation at its best. It benefits delegator and delegatee.

Tasks Remain for You and Me

There is yet one more observation I'd like for us to make about the subject of delegating.

It is interesting to note that although Jesus touched and healed countless people during His years of earthly ministry, when He ascended from this globe to return to His Father, disease, tragedy, deformities, dysfunction and death still existed. While He walked this earth He didn't heal all the sick, He didn't raise all the dead, He didn't open all blinded eyes or deaf ears.

In Acts 3 we read of a lame man who was a regular, recognized beggar in the temple courts . . . courts Jesus had presumably passed through on many occasions. Yet, the responsibility of bringing physical healing to this man was reserved for Peter and John, the leaders of Jesus' fledgling church. Reading on through the chapter, we realize that this man's public healing opened a remarkable opportunity for Peter and John to testify to the truth of the gospel of Jesus Christ before an open-minded throng of witnesses. Could Jesus have healed that man earlier? Of course; but He didn't. Instead, He left this as one of the many tasks to be completed by His people, His church.

To each of us He left a series of important tasks to fulfill. I like the way the apostle Paul explained our individual responsibility in God's kingdom:

> For it is by grace you have been saved, through faith—and this not from yourselves, it is the gift of God—not by works, so that no one can boast. For we are God's workmanship, created in Christ Jesus to do good works, which God prepared in advance for us to do. (Ephesians 2:8-10)

So, our salvation does not depend on our doing enough good things (we couldn't possibly do enough good to counter our sin). It is a gift offered to each of us freely, right from God's hand. But the good works are something we are created to do, with God's help. He prepared them in advance. As we've said before, knowing our individual and innate limitations, strengths and preferences, the Creator prepared us for the work and the work for us.

Our salvation does not depend on our doing enough good things (we couldn't possibly do enough good to counter our sin). It is a gift offered to each of us freely, right from God's hand.

For some it is raising children or being a cheering section for a spouse or being responsible in the workplace for the livelihoods of dozens of people. Your task will be different than mine. Take a look at Hebrews 12:1:

> Therefore, since we are surrounded by such a great cloud of witnesses, let us throw off everything that hinders and the sin that so easily entangles, and let us run with perseverance the race marked out for us.

Note that it is not the race marked out for someone else, but the race marked out for each one of us. You do your work and I'll do mine. I'll cheer you on and I'd love to hear your voice cheering for me.

Challenge of the Week

For a helpful "perspective check," read the case Job makes before God in Job 30:20-31:40. Jot down your own concerns about what's going on in your life and in the lives of those around you. Then re-read God's reply to His servant in Job 38-41. Journal your response to God's eternal and wide-ranging perspective.

Myth: If I used to be able to make time for a particular task, I must always be able to make time for it.

When I was five years old, my grandmother, three of my aunts, two uncles and two cousins moved from unpredictable Chicago to always-balmy South Florida. In those early years after their move, I remember talking with them by phone and hearing them decry the lack of flagrant seasonal changes in the South. They said they missed autumn most of all. (However, what they never seemed to miss was the opportunity of gloating about running their air conditioning in the middle of February.)

As for me, I've never minded Chicago, which is known by natives for its two (not four) seasons: snow and construction. In mid-January I might beg to reevaluate the idea of moving to Florida, but generally I enjoy the lemony greens of a northern springtime, the translucent jades of mid-summer, the mellow chocolates of autumn. I've even been known to find beauty in icicles coating power lines after a November sleet-storm or in seeing crimson winter berries poking their noses through evergreen tips frosted with a fresh coat of glistening snow.

I think it is more than the secret poet in my soul that makes me appreciate the patterns and the flow of changing seasons. The seasons' changes, after all, bespeak the creativity of the Creator, the consistency of His workings on our behalf and the eternally symbolic cycle that brings life and death and the promise of life again.

But for all of the poetic aspects of changing seasons in nature, when it comes to my own life, I'd much prefer the lulling sameness of a Floridian winter to the chaotic changes of a northern season cycle. I'd prefer it, but alas I seldom receive it. For life, yours and mine, is made up of its own series of seasons: the carefree, toy-strewn springtime of early childhood; the mounting intensity of the education years; the encumbering responsibility of the work years; the quest for significance and usefulness in the post-retirement years. There are seasons of singleness and marriage, of childrearing and empty nesting, of first apartments and nursing homes, of gathering and dispersing.

These seasons may come in a different sequence or at a later time for you than they will for me. Some of us may skip certain seasons entirely (out of our own choosing or because of the path God has chosen for us to follow). The only predictability of life's seasons is that they will be constantly changing. It has been so since the first family took up residence outside Eden. The author of Ecclesiastes took note of the cadence of the seasons in his oft-quoted passage:

> There is a time for everything,
>   and a season for every activity under heaven:
>   a time to be born and a time to die,
>   a time to plant and a time to uproot,
>   a time to kill and a time to heal,
>   a time to tear down and a time to build,
>   a time to weep and a time to laugh,
>   a time to mourn and a time to dance,
>   a time to scatter stones and a time to gather them,
>   a time to embrace and a time to refrain,
>   a time to search and a time to give up,

a time to keep and a time to throw away,
a time to tear and a time to mend,
a time to be silent and a time to speak,
a time to love and a time to hate,
a time for war and a time for peace. (Ecclesiastes 3:1-8)

People—bosses, friends, colleagues, even family members—will move in and out of our lives. Our roles in their lives will be ever-changing—at times we may be solely responsible for them (as with nurturing tiny tots or caring for elderly relatives), other times they may seem not to need anything from us at all.

With the changing seasons may come the inclination toward exuberance at one extreme—when we feel invincible, full of energy, ready to take on any challenge—and sullen grieving at the next moment—when lifting our heads off a pillow requires every last ounce of mustered energy. This is life's symphony—God's gift to keep us growing and awake and dependent upon His provision.

While seasons bring internal and external changes to our lives, they also bring with them their own special sets of demands.

Why this soliloquy on life's changing seasons in a book about ordering our lives by God's priority system? Because while seasons bring internal and external changes to our lives, they also bring with them their own special sets of demands. The demands upon a self-supporting single adult are different (although no less rigorous) than those upon a stay-at-home mom with a newborn and two toddlers in tow. Likewise, the tasks we have come to expect ourselves to be able to accomplish on a regular basis in one season of life may be unattainable, even undesirable, in another season.

Tradeoffs and Choices

Yesterday afternoon, while preparing to teach my college students a unit in classic fiction, I reread one of the most famous opening lines in all of literature:

> It was the best of times, it was the worst of times, it was the age of wisdom, it was the age of foolishness, it was the epoch of belief, it was the epoch of incredulity, it was the season of Light, it was the season of Darkness, it was the spring of hope, it was the winter of despair.
> —Charles Dickens, *A Tale of Two Cities*

What struck me as I read this passage was more than Dickens' clever word plays and poetic structure (although those are significant to my students' lessons). Rather, it was the insightful juxtaposition of best and worst, belief and unbelief, hope and despair. Each of the seasons of our lives holds both joys and sorrows, both challenges and delights.

Over and over as we've examined the subject of making the best use of our time, we've acknowledged that we are called to make difficult choices about what's good, what's better and what's best. It wouldn't be so difficult if we were choosing between bad and good, but the good-better-best kinds of choices are particularly frustrating. Ignoring my human frailties, I'd choose to fit them all—good, better and best—into my plans. But back in chapter 1 I described for you a time when doing it all got the best of me.

Way back in graduate school I learned the important lessons of setting my priorities and taking my stand behind them in defending my tough choices. I learned them, but I don't always remember to apply them. It was only a matter of months after my grad-school health meltdown that I failed the time management test of good, better, best. Here's how it unfolded:

A Room Full of Third Graders

When I returned home to Chicago after six years out of state completing my undergraduate and graduate degrees, my family's circumstances had changed. My grandfather (our pastor) had succumbed to a slow and difficult death. My family was worshiping in a new congregation where I knew no one, and where everyone my age was married (most with several children). My high school friends had dispersed to various states. My season had changed. Life as I had known it six years earlier was no more.

I recognized that becoming involved in the church family would be key to my resettling process in this new season of independent single adulthood. So, I made an effort to be involved, walking through every door open to me. When one of the women of the church called to ask me to teach Sunday school to third graders, I didn't hesitate for a moment. I heartily agreed. After all, several years before I had taught Vacation Bible School to girls in that same age group and had thoroughly enjoyed the week. But one week of VBS and an entire term of co-ed Sunday school are two different things.

That first morning I showed up brimming with enthusiasm. But by the time the hour was over and I stumbled into the sanctuary, I felt drained, spent and discouraged. Clearly, this was not the time for me to teach children in the Sunday school setting. At the end of the year, I gave up teaching and stopped attending the Sunday school hour altogether.

About that time a new friend asked me to try her church. The moment I stepped in the door, I felt I belonged. There were other single twenty-something professionals. Some taught Sunday school, but others served on church boards and played key roles in various church ministries. Eventually, I became a board member myself, then a co-teacher for the single adult

Sunday school class, a member of the choir and a vocalist on the worship team.

This is what I mean by good, better, best and how these shift about in the various seasons of life. In the summer of my college season, it was easy for me to take on a week of VBS. I left my work behind me every night when I picked up my purse and walked out into the parking lot. My best friend (who was getting her degree in early childhood education) taught in the room beside me, and we studied curriculum together, shared hearty laughs over the funny things the kids said, even combined the classes at times during the week.

But after graduate school, I assumed a demanding role as a media spokesperson for a major corporation. I was regularly quoted on the front page of Chicago newspapers and often was an impromptu guest on live radio and TV broadcasts. I traveled periodically on business and spent many sleepless nights fielding questions from reporters on the overnight beat looking to drum up stories where there were none. My stress level and exhaustion were overwhelming.

Certainly teaching Sunday school to third graders is a noble task. I thank God for the women in my childhood whom He gifted to teach me during my primary school years. I still remember their names. Alongside the marvelous example my parents provided, these women had a profound impact on my knowledge and understanding of Scripture. The example these women set for me was one of the reasons I was so eager to teach the children myself. But, God did not gift me with the inner skills and abilities to do the task well at that season of my life.

We'll discuss finding, honing and using our gifts in chapter 11, but for now let me make this observation: When I bowed out, I freed up the position for the creative, energetic woman who was gifted to work with eight-year-olds. I also freed my time to use the gifts I do have in the church productively—gifts that energize, rather than drain, me. Everyone won when I aligned my choices with the priorities God established for that season of my life.

This is a lesson whose wisdom I've recently seen in operation in the life of Cheryl, one of the apprentice writers I mentor through the Jerry B. Jenkins Christian Writers Guild. She's in a brief season of over-commitment and is looking for some momentary relief of pressure. Here's Cheryl's apt description of her situation:

> Over the past week, we put our house on the market and cleaned out the clutter. We are in the process of buying a big, old farmhouse with lots of character. I have been over there quite a bit with the renovators. I am still working full time and filling in for another girl who is off with carpal tunnel syndrome. In addition, I am trying to find time to get my boys ready for going back to school. Jeff grew about five inches this summer, and all his pants are way too short now. . . .
>
> I feel like I'm sliding down a mountain full speed, and I can't catch my breath.

The moment I began reading that paragraph, I started to feel out of breath in sympathy for her. So, when she asked, specifically and thoughtfully, for relief in this season, I was more than inclined to agree with her plan. She wrote:

> I was wondering if I could take this week's lesson off and hand it in when the next one is due. I know it will put me two weeks behind, but once school starts and we get back into a semi-normal routine, I will find time to catch up.

Here is a person who understands the limitations of each season of life, and is willing to work within the confines set by each season, without sacrificing goals and dreams in the process.

Season of Carpentry

I feel guilty and not a little disappointed when I can't say yes to the good things of life. So, here again, I look to the life of Jesus Christ for direction and encouragement.

After Jesus' birth and dedication in the Temple, we see only a few more scenes of His pre-ministry season on earth. In fact, the Gospel writer Luke sums up this season in just a few words: "And Jesus grew in wisdom and stature, and in favor with God and men" (2:52). We know that Jesus submitted to His parents' authority during this growing-up season, and we also know that He learned and plied the trade of carpentry, presumably from Joseph. Since He was known by the locals as "the carpenter" (Mark 6:3) we might easily infer that He was a master craftsman, known for His quality workmanship. Certainly He would have spent much time watching His carpenter father, using the tools side-by-side, listening to clients and learning to meet their expectations in His work. He did this for a season of life, up until the approximate age of thirty.

God seldom wastes an opportunity in anyone's life.

But then things changed. His season of ministry burst into full bloom and He left behind the tools of carpentry to traverse the countryside seeking lost souls. Was His season of carpentry one of biding time until the real work began? Somehow, knowing that God seldom wastes an opportunity in anyone's life, I doubt that this season was wasted. I also doubt, however, that Jesus felt guilty for not taking on more carpentry projects during His ministry season.

When His season changed yet again, as the time for His sacrifice on our behalf loomed large on the horizon, we read in the

Living Bible: "As the time drew near for his return to heaven, he moved steadily onward toward Jerusalem with an iron will" (Luke 9:51, TLB). Once again, priorities changed, obligations took on a new color and Jesus moved ahead into the new season wholeheartedly, with an iron will, ready to accomplish every task the Father called Him to do.

Faithful in Few Things

Jesus as much as told us to expect these same changing seasons in our twenty-first-century lives. In His parable of the three stewards entrusted to invest their master's assets, Jesus emphatically tells the faithful two: "Well done, good and faithful servant! You have been faithful with a few things; I will put you in charge of many things. Come and share your master's happiness!" (Matthew 25:21). So our faithfulness in the early seasons of life when we are entrusted with a few assets for use in God's kingdom is the prerequisite to the possibility of our being entrusted with greater assets at later seasons.

It's a principle that carries through from the Old Testament as well. God encouraged His fearless workman, Zerubbabel, with this statement: "Do not despise these small beginnings, for the LORD rejoices to see the work begin" (Zechariah 4:10, NLT). In his commentary on this verse, Matthew Henry wrote,

> Though the beginnings be small, God can make the latter end greatly to increase; a grain of mustard-seed may become a great tree. Let not the dawning light be despised, for it will shine more and more to the perfect day. The day of small things is the day of precious things, and will be the day of great things.[1]

When we are entrusted with investing a few talents, with a seemingly insignificant beginning, it may be a test to see whether we are prepared for the next step.

Letting Others Learn Too

But there is a logical implication to all of this exciting growth in responsibilities. We must realize that when we are entrusted with the new task, we may reasonably expect it to become necessary for us to relinquish the initial task to someone else.

I had a wonderfully talented professor in graduate school. She was so gifted in the classroom that I can still quote many of the lessons I learned under her tutelage. However, she was also a gifted motivator of people and a trustworthy leader. So she was promoted up through the ranks, higher and higher up the administrative ladder. As this happened, she spent less and less time in the classroom until she reached the level where she could no longer carry a regular teaching load. She has entered a new season of life. And she is neither shirking her responsibility nor misusing her gifts. Instead she is allowing others to be equipped for their life tasks through carrying the teaching load, a service her predecessors once provided for her.

Hopes and Expectations

The biggest lesson I've learned from acknowledging the changing seasons of my life is that while I can hope to please everyone and say yes to every good opportunity, I am free to relax my expectations of myself—for I am my own worst critic.

For example, I had a little run-in with my own expectations this week. It happens that one of the hazards of a Chicago winter is an annual grudge match with a head cold. I've been caught in this nuisance battle for the last six days. Now, I'm not seeking your sympathy (although I would plead with you not to make any disparaging remarks about my nose looking like Rudolph's or my voice sounding like Kermit the Frog's or my hair looking like Don King's). However, due to the cold season I find my physical strength and concentration limited by frequent interruptions of sneezes and wheezes. I can't expect myself to keep up my usual quick pace in writing, in e-mail responses, in choir practice attendance or even in housekeeping. It would be unreasonable and unproductive to try to force myself to keep up the pace I'd originally planned for this week.

I've had to spin off some good things—lunch with a friend, getting ahead on a project not due for two weeks, etc. I've had to readjust others—as in finding a way to teach my Tuesday morning English class while my vocal chords are in rebellion. Funny that I've been writing this chapter this week—it's been a providential reminder to me. So, with these lessons firmly in hand, I'll allow a few whines and whimpers to escape my lips; then I'll settle back on my pillows, curl up in my warm pjs and grab for a new box of extra soft tissues.

Challenge of the Week

Read Luke 9-11, looking for the way Jesus looked head-on at the limitations of His time on earth. Pay special attention to the increased urgency in His preparation of His followers for what was to come. Record your observations below or in your journal.

Endnote

1. *Matthew Henry's Commentary on the Whole Bible*, Electronic Edition: Zechariah 4:1-10, p. 14.

Myth: Rest, relaxation and retreating from the crowd
are luxuries I'll never be able to afford.

I had just finished preparing my students' final exam. It had been a long and difficult semester; preparing the exam set off an internal review of all that had happened during the previous three months. A torrent of exasperation, disappointment and disillusionment flooded my mind, but I had to cram these feelings and send them back to where they came from, because next on the agenda was an important writing assignment with a deadline I couldn't afford to miss.

Just then, the electricity went out. Never fear. I switched to my auxiliary portable computer and called up the proper file; I was back in business. One floor below me I heard the buzz of power tools morph into the tap, tap, tap, pow of manual labor (workmen are installing ceramic tile below my office). Their power is out too.

As I said, I opened the file, sat still and waited for inspiration to strike. Except it didn't. It wasn't writer's block, exactly. It was more like an overwhelming disquiet suppressing my inner writer's voice. The battery-operated clock tick, tick, ticked away in monotonous tedium, reminding me by each movement of the hand that my humming computer has only two hours of battery life—and I was losing precious writing time every second I squandered staring at the blank screen.

The more I focused on the incessant ticking of the clock, the less ready to write I felt. I wasn't procrastinating; I was determined to write. But I couldn't squeeze the words from my brain down to my fingers.

Finally, I shuffled over to my reading chair, beside which I keep several devotional books. I picked up a pretty little volume I'd received as a gift. It features colorful renderings of artist Thomas Kinkade's paintings mingled with daily inspirations written by Welsh pastor Selwyn Hughes.

Inner disquiet had revealed itself for what it was—the mortal enemy of productivity—but it proved no match for the refreshment found in restful moments spent with God.

During the next half hour, I read six or seven of Hughes' soothing devotional thoughts. I wasn't affected so much by the subject matter as by the calming, quieting silence of meditating on God's Word. As my inner disquiet receded, words began to snap to attention in my mind, and I rushed back to the computer to begin to unleash them on my keyboard.

Inner disquiet had revealed itself for what it was—the mortal enemy of productivity—but it proved no match for the refreshment found in restful moments spent with God. For this reason if for no other, our time ordering study would be incomplete were we not to explode the myth that restful, quiet moments are luxury rather than necessity for our minds and our bodies. In chapter 3 we talked about retreating and spending time alone with the Lord, but the brand of rest we'll discuss in this chapter goes a step further. It involves an inner peacefulness that does not depend upon those events circling around us. It doesn't require us to "get alone" or "get away from it all." Rather it requires the pursuit of God's soothing, calm voice to sustain us in the middle of our active lives.

In Search of a Rested Spirit

I must confess to you that this chapter has proven most difficult for me to write, because this is the myth that gives me the hardest time. Back in the '80s (yes, the 1980s) when I first heard the phrase "Type-A Person" I might just as well have seen my picture beside it in the dictionary: the definition was made for me.

I am so Type-A that I used to sleep with a pad of paper and pen beside my bed. I say "used to" because I've graduated: I now sleep with my palm-sized computer beside my bed—and can write (or even dictate) long dissertations in its dim light any time, day or night. After all, you never know when the perfect solution to the day's problems will present itself. Seize the moment; that's always been my refrain.

Chaos cannot snuff out true rest.

Another symptom of Type-A-ness is the fact that many of us don't know the meaning of a 100 percent restful vacation. It's not that we don't schedule vacations, but we always seem to infuse them with work. For example, I'll go to Florida in February and write half of a book manuscript while sitting on a balcony overlooking the Bay, be a guest speaker for a single adults Sunday school class and visit several Christian bookstores to promote my books—all in eleven days. Or, someone else may fly to California, spend one quiet hour by the pool and then the remainder of the week hold teleconferences, study spreadsheets and keep hourly tabs on his office staff via voicemail and e-mail.

It's not that we don't know the right thing to do. We *know* it, but *applying* it is another story entirely. We are in search of rest and yet are disinclined to allow ourselves to practice it.

The Master of the Calm

Rest. It is an endangered commodity in this chaotic twenty-first century. And yet, chaos cannot snuff out true rest. Don't believe me? If you have a Bible nearby, take a quick read through Mark 4:36-41. It is the story of Jesus and His disciples in a boat in the middle of a storm. The disciples respond to the storm just as I would—with disquiet and fear, straining at the oars, trying to survive the situation with brute strength bolstered by huge surges of adrenaline. Their spirits are in an agitated state that is the antithesis of rest.

Jesus, on the other hand, well let's read how He responds in verse 38: "Jesus was in the stern, sleeping on a cushion." It's always bugged me that Jesus could be so calm, so at rest, in the middle of a storm. While He's enjoying a cushy, comfortable sleep, the boat is being swamped with squalls and assaulted by violent air currents. When the petrified disciples finally succeed in rousing the Master, He stands, looks around, tells the waves to be quiet and sits back down—reproaching the disciples for their lack of faith.

> Until I am still and quiet and at rest before
> the God of the universe, I am unable
> to tune in to His frequency.

It shouldn't surprise us that Jesus is calm *in* a storm, and that He can bring calm *to* a storm. It shouldn't surprise us because the God of the Old Testament is also surrounded by a calm. Consider how God showed Himself to the prophet Elijah.

> The LORD said, "Go out and stand on the mountain in the presence of the LORD, for the LORD is about to pass by."
>
> Then a great and powerful wind tore the mountains apart and shattered the rocks before the LORD, but the LORD was not in the wind. After the wind there was an earthquake, but the LORD was not in the earthquake. After the earthquake came a fire, but the LORD was not in the fire. And after the fire came a gentle whisper. When Elijah heard it, he pulled his cloak over his face and went out and stood at the mouth of the cave.
>
> Then a voice said to him, "What are you doing here, Elijah?" (1 Kings 19:11-13)

When He appeared to Elijah, God allowed the shattering wind and the earthquake and the fire to precede Him, but He Himself was in the calm, not in the chaos. And it wasn't until the quiet came that His gentle whisper was evident. Had it been there all along? Was it simply overshadowed by the cacophony of circumstances? Was it drowned out by disquiet—from without and within? These are questions we don't have the information to answer in Elijah's case. But I have experienced the truth firsthand, and have found that until I am still and quiet and at rest before the God of the universe, I am unable to tune in to His frequency. And the inability to take a breather, brought on by the extremity of my Type-A personality, makes this quiet listening stance most difficult for me.

A Model of Retreating

We often read in the Gospels about Jesus making a way to "get away" from the crowds and demands and pressures of His very public ministry. We've already covered the fact that Jesus often went alone to quiet places to commune with His Father. But Jesus also made restful time a priority for His disciples. For example, the *Nelson Study Bible*, in its comments on Mark 2:13, says, "Jesus regularly taught the multitudes in retreat settings. This is indicated by the continuous tense of the verbs used here: They kept on coming, and Jesus kept on teaching." In fact, the Gospel of Mark is packed with scenes when Jesus made important revelations to His disciples in times when He had taken them away from the hustle and press of the crowd. In 3:13-15 we read that after teaching the crowds, "Jesus went up on a mountain and called the ones he wanted to go with him. And they came to him. Then he selected twelve of them to be his regular companions, calling them apostles. He sent them out to preach, and he gave them authority to cast out demons" (NLT). Once again we see that Jesus took them aside together to call and equip them, away from the distractions of their everyday lives.

The Believer's Study Bible makes this observation in its article titled, "The Foundation of The Church (Matthew 16:13-22)":

> In the latter part of His ministry Jesus observed a series of retreats with the Twelve. On the last of these retreats His purpose was to discern whether or not the Twelve understood Him and His mission. This last retreat ended at Caesarea Philippi, a northern Gentile city which housed the oldest and newest centers of pagan worship. . . . In the midst of these idolatries, old and new, Peter confessed of Jesus, "You are the Christ, the Son of the living God" (Matthew 16:16). This confession became the foundation of the church.[1]

But the most telling retreat, to me, is the one the Father planned for Jesus *and* His closest followers in the middle of the final week of the Savior's earthly ministry. John 12 notes that Jesus left Jerusalem and got away to spend the night in the home of his friends Martha, Mary and Lazarus in the nearby sleepy burg of

Bethany. There He was respected and treated with the dignity befitting His position; He was loved and comforted in the presence of His trusted friends; He was honored with a dinner and graciously received the soothing ministry of Mary who anointed Him with costly perfume. There, amongst His trusted companions and friends, He who was about to perform the ultimate ministry for humankind received ministry to His own body lavished by His devoted follower. And there He found a peaceful respite, even while the ultimate storm was battering down the door.

These are some of the many benefits of taking time away from the pressures of life—to get alone with God or apart with our fellow journeyers, to spend moments in prayer or receive with grace the unselfish ministry of those who love us.

Finding What Makes You Rest

As I mentioned in chapter 3, often when we are grouchy and grumpy and downright inconsolable, a time-out is exactly what is best for us. It can be a reward, not a reprimand. Imagine that you are in need of a time-out—perhaps you even need one right now. If you had unlimited resources at your disposal, what kind of retreat would you choose? For some it would be the retreat of spending quality time reconnecting with family and friends; for others it would be the retreat of silence and aloneness (notice I didn't say loneliness, but rather *aloneness*, which connotes peace and a desired time apart from other people). Maybe your retreat would be a long walk, renting a cabin or spending the day in a local retreat facility. Maybe it's watching a favorite old movie or TV show or sneaking in a few moments with a magazine and a cup of cocoa while the baby naps.

When I was interviewing professional women for my book *Staying True in a World of Lies*, several of them broached the subject of de-stressing or relaxing as a necessary part of their organizational success. I used many of those quotes in the book, but a few of them bear repeating.

Elizabeth, a high-school administrator, offered a good perspective on those daily rest periods that are critical to our emotional health:

> On the days when I come home aggravated, I take a half hour to myself, sit back and look at something else to change the tone of my day. I might read. Or sit peacefully. Eventually it all calms down. Sometimes it reappears the next day. But I try to remind myself that a week from now this problem will be over and probably forgotten. (pp. 154-155)

Similarly, accountant Joan mentioned that on many occasions right in the middle of an exceptionally stressful day she has gone into her private office, left the lights off, put her head in her hands and prayed for guidance. This, she said, would provide a short-term emotional release. However, often the concerns of the day would come back to haunt her when she would try to find sleep. So, she developed a restful nighttime routine many of her fellow Type-A folks might want to emulate:

> Because I can't come home and just turn off all of the hectic chaos of the day, I have learned that Bible reading, even if it means just carving out five or ten minutes, helps me calm down before I go to bed. I subscribe to several magazines, including *Guideposts* and *Leadership*. Reading these before I go to bed helps too. I prop myself up on a big pillow, turn on the indoor waterfall my kids bought me for Christmas, put a symphonic CD into the stereo and read from the Bible or one of these magazines, so that the last thing I'm thinking about before I go to sleep is God-centered. The sound of the waterfall is soothing; the Scripture reminders

put life in the right perspective for me. These things taken together calm me so I can sleep peacefully. (p. 154)

Scheduling peaceful times regularly—and I do mean actually adding them (in ink) to our planners and guarding them as we would any other appointment—is a cherished necessity that will build up our overall emotional well-being.

I've modified Joan's prescription to fit my own preferences. When I'm desperate for a brief time-out, what works for me is the mood created by flavored coffee, dim light, a home decorating magazine, a Mozart CD and a long soak in my Jacuzzi tub. These small things work wonders for my concentration, productivity and overall attitude. But when I need a more prolonged time-out, I enjoy a trip to Green Lake, a Christian retreat center midway up the state of Wisconsin, about four hours' drive from my home. There I can wander through acres of wooded property, listening to the crunch of snow or the rustle of leaves or the lulling swish of the waves on the lake. Something about being away from technology and returning to the romance of nature (without giving up necessities like indoor plumbing and electricity to run my blow dryer) recharges my emotional and spiritual batteries.

Scheduling peaceful times regularly—and I do mean actually adding them (in ink) to our planners and guarding them as we would any other appointment—is a cherished necessity that will build up our overall emotional well-being. I've seen that when I make an intentional effort to schedule time-outs in my busy schedule to do whatever provides me with refreshment and enjoyment, I find my productivity multiplied in the ensuing work time.

Meditating Moments Meet Needs

Let me offer a final observation on the subject before we
close our discussion. I've told this story in speaking engagements and even briefly mentioned it in my book *Praying Like
Jesus*, but it bears repeating in this context.

> Retreating at its most fulfilling means setting aside
> time not only for my own refreshment, but more
> importantly, for the refilling of my spirit from the
> deep and refreshing waters of the Spirit of God.

As a speaker or an attender I've been on dozens of seasonal retreats. Most of them have smushed into one lumpy and generic
memory: we arrive late at night after the upstream battle of Friday
night traffic. In the morning we'd like to take a nature walk but are
instead conscripted into listening to someone (sometimes it is I)
speak for way too long as we gaze yearningly at the placid lake just
outside a window (oh to dip one little toe into the crystal waters),
but by the time the speaker is finished it's nearly time to trudge
back home again.

However, one singles' retreat I attended more than ten years
ago deviated from the norm. It started much the same as others
have, but when the clock struck 11 on Saturday morning, the
speaker, writer and musician John Fischer, stopped speaking. He
asked us to open our Bibles to a certain passage (I wish I could remember what passage it was, but that fact is lost in the recesses of
my memory) and instructed us to read until we heard God's voice
quickening a passage in our hearts. He said it could be just a few
verses or many chapters,but to be sure to stop and meditate on
whatever God showed us. The rules were that we were to find a
private reading spot in the scenic outdoors of the retreat complex,

and that we were not to say a word to another person until the lunch bell rang an hour later.

That hour impacted my life as few single hours ever have. It taught me the important lesson that retreating at its most fulfilling means setting aside time not only for my own refreshment, but more importantly, for the refilling of my spirit from the deep and refreshing waters of the Spirit of God.

Challenge of the Week

Rather than recommending a specific Bible passage, let me suggest that you pick up your favorite study Bible, open it to the place where you last read and do what I did on that retreat: read silently until you can hear God speaking directly to you right from the pages of His holy Word. Then stop, prayerfully ask Him what He's trying to tell you, journal your thoughts and act on His direction—whatever it proves to be. I'll be praying that you will hear His voice clearly and powerfully.

Endnote

1. "The Foundation of The Church (Matthew 16:13-22)," *Believer's Study Bible*. Copyright © 1991 by the Criswell Center for Biblical Studies. Special Study Helps, copyright © 1991, 1990, 1985, 1983, 1975 by Thomas Nelson, Inc. Electronic Edition STEP Files copyright © 1998, Parsons Technology, Inc., all rights reserved.

Myth: Those who scream the loudest require
my attention the most.

As much as this book has been about conquering the indiscriminate spending (or squandering) of time, it has also become a book of recognizing and making choices. It is in a review of how we handle the time factor that we can obtain an unmistakable snapshot of our priorities and the choices we've made either intentionally or, more likely, by default. These choices determine which voices we heed and which we ignore. When they affect those we love, these choices can have eternal consequences.

> It is in a review of our time usage that we can obtain an unmistakable snapshot of our priorities and the choices we've made either intentionally or, more likely, by default.

Before you continue reading, take a few moments to inventory your own time usage for the last week or, even better, the last month. Consider the choices that are evident in the way you've spent your time. Which choices had eternity potential? In other words, which choices would ultimately make a difference if all materialism, ulterior motives and earth-bound needs were stripped away? Now, as you read this chapter, keep your own choices in mind.

101

Two Commonplace Snapshots

Lest you be tempted to accuse me of being melodramatic with all this talk about eternal values in daily life, allow me to share two real-life scenarios in which real people had to make tough calls—choosing between good and better, between the tasks that screamed for their attention and the people who needed their loving care.

Scenario One

Joyce was planning a dinner party for eight couples. She was well known in the church for her elaborate settings, her gourmet menus, her down-to-the-millisecond orchestration of every aspect of the evening. With one hand she was stirring the orange glaze to top the Cornish hens, which (by the way) were plumply stuffed and browning nicely in the top oven. With the other hand she was reaching into the freezer to grab for her home-packed ice cream cake, which was ready to receive its next colorful layer (pistachio, if you must know). With one eye she surveyed the dining table, set with her fine silver, china and crystal. With the other eye Joyce watched her little girl who was amusing herself with her dolly in the backyard. Suddenly the little girl ran into the kitchen, breathless. "Mommy, Mommy," she insisted, reaching out a hand to grip her mother's forearm. "Come quick! A rainbow, Mommy. Jesus put a rainbow in the sky over the yard!"

Joyce had a choice—would she turn off the burner, follow her daughter out the door to see the rainbow and capture the teachable moment to talk about the first rainbow? Or was her dinner party so important that she would choose to forego a bonding opportunity with her little girl?

Scenario Two

Kurt and Pam were in the car with six-year-old Ethan after church one Sunday morning. Kurt was listening to a music tape as they placed their order at the chicken restaurant's drive-thru window. The song playing was one that received a great deal of radio play that year; it asked the rather frivolous (if not hilarious) question: What would happen if cartoon characters got saved? Kurt was learning the song to teach it to the Vacation Bible School children at the church the following week. Typically, the bright young Ethan mastered the song well before his father did. He actually had become quite fond of it and loved to sing along, enjoying the idea of his favorite cartoon characters in a "Jesus song."

Kurt was intent and focused on learning the song; his purpose was a good and time-sensitive one. And yet, he soon became aware of God's quiet voice prompting him to seize the teachable moment with Ethan. What choice would he make?

I'll let you in on the choices Joyce and Kurt made later. For now, let's consider the problem tough calls like these can create for diligent and orderly individuals.

Making the Right Call

Today I blew it. I let the urgent (the writing of this chapter) blow away the important (my mom needed me to make a decision about whether or not I could fit a particular dining cart into my spare bedroom). What mom really needed was my time and attention, and I—being two chapters behind where I had planned to be at this date—put the completion of my chapter ahead of her needs. When she called me on the intercom, I informed her it was a decision I couldn't make today, and asked if she could wait until another day to arrange her dining room with or without the cart. In my defense (we always have a good defense, don't we?), it is rather embarrassing to attend a Christmas party with my friends from church (as I did last evening), to have them ask how my new book is coming and to be obliged out of truthfulness to admit to being behind schedule on a *time management* book, of all things. But, despite my rationalization, I made a questionable call.

Too often those things that scream the loudest and demand the most of us eat up all our quality time. If any time or energy is left for the things that are truly important to us—a child's first rainbow or answering an inquiry about Jesus or helping Mother with a decorating dilemma—we offer them what's left over, a mangled scrap tossed off the banquet table of our time.

Too often those things that scream the loudest and demand the most of us eat up all our quality time.

The screaming I hear resounding in my ears today is emanating from some ink which I used six months ago to sign my name, promising to deliver this book by January 30. And yes, the book will most likely be finished by that date, regardless of whether I move the cart into my spare room today or not. But, as I say, too often the things that scream the loudest aren't the most important—they may be *urgent* here and now, but they may not be the highest on my eternity-minded priority list. After all, what comes with me into eternity? Is it money? An orderly office? An inventory log listing all the books I've written and sold? Certainly not. All of those things stay behind on earth. The types of things that make it to eternity with me are the relationships I've built with loved ones, the memories of the value I've placed on all the people I encounter and the results of all the energy I've spent encouraging others toward godliness.

Am I saying that deadlines are not important? Or that we ought not consider clients' or bosses' needs when making our choices? Certainly not. We can't make every concession or place every other person's needs ahead of our own. There are some earthbound needs that are pretty important—my favorites are eating and living indoors, to be frank. But those of us who tend toward workaholism or perfectionism can miss the really good stuff of life while we are focusing on accumulating for ourselves a multitude of things that will eventually rust, fade or disintegrate in a cloud of dust.

The Pharisees of Life

At every juncture in this book so far, we've found something in our study of Jesus' example that was relevant to our discussion. This topic offers no exception. As He walked the earth doing good deeds for people of high and low estate, Jesus was challenged by many of the same choices we face. While His heart went out to everyday men and women who were hurting, who were ensnared by sin, who were enmeshed in the agony of death and disease, His ears could not help but resound with the loud public spectacle the religious rulers of His day made all around Him.

They were called Pharisees and Sadducees. They were scholars of the old covenant, meticulous to a fault in following their strict and often skewed interpretations of the law God laid down to Moses and the wandering Israelites millennia before. Scrupulous in their outward actions, yet pompous and power hungry in their hearts, these men constantly grilled Jesus with questions designed to sidetrack, discredit or trip Him up.

On occasion Jesus made the calculated choice to speak directly to the Pharisees. Sometimes it was to silence their incessant questions (you can read examples of the expert answers He gave them in Mark 3:1-6 and John 8:1-11). Other times it was publicly, to put His finger directly on the pulse of their radical religiosity (Matthew 23:27 where He called them whitewashed tombs or John 8:44 where He called them sons of the devil, for example).

In general the Pharisees made the loudest public spectacle of themselves, but Jesus saved His softest words and most gentle one-on-one attention for the men and women who most needed and desired His touch. He explained this choice to us in Mark 2:17, when He said, "It is not the healthy who need a doctor, but the sick." In other words, those yelling the loudest would seek to drown out the labored prayers of those teetering on the tenuous brink of eternity. But He would not allow the quiet calls to be overcome by the cacophony of raging crowd noise.

Consider your own reading about Jesus' life and ponder this question: With whom did He spend most of His limited time and energy?

- A rag-tag group of twelve misfits (fishermen, revolutionaries and tax collectors were among these ranks; see Matthew 4:18-22, 9:9-10, etc.),
- an outcast woman who chose to draw water from the city's well in the blazing heat of midday rather than chance meeting other townswomen drawing in the cool of the morning (see John 4:7-26),
- and one particular religious leader named Nicodemus who came quietly, at night, apart from the crowd, with unadulterated and legitimate questions for the Master (see John 3:1-21).

These are the individuals, the genuine seekers, on whom Jesus lavished His eternal insights, His best energies, His quality time. When He was with them, He focused on them and their needs: framing truths in language they would understand, meeting them eye-to-eye, working beside them shoulder-to-shoulder, fulfilling their physical and spiritual longings with the gentle touch of His hand.

Getting Everything into Focus

When Jesus was alone with His disciples, He focused on them: answering their questions when they didn't understand a parable He had told the crowd earlier (Matthew 13:18-23); anticipating their needs as He did when He washed their feet on the evening before His crucifixion (John 13:4-17); allowing them a glimpse of His eternal glory, as He did when He allowed His inner circle to see Him transfigured into a glowing figure on a mountaintop (Matthew 17:1-2).

When something is important to us, it warrants our focused and undivided attention.

From this example we can see modeled before us a solid time-management principle that we would be well-served to apply to our own daily schedules: When something is important to us, it warrants our focused and undivided attention. I apply this to my work life by having only one project folder open on my desk at any one time. If I'm working on this book, I'm not thinking about the article I'm writing for a magazine, printing my Christmas letter or answering my telephone. When I've made the choice to spend my time on this book, I am focused on it and nothing else. When I've made the choice to focus on someone or something else in my life, I give that person or task the same undivided attention.

This means when I'm attending a social gathering and a friend needs to share a prayer concern with me, I'm not keeping one eye on her while the other eye scans the crowd for someone more intriguing or beneficial to my status. I communicate that I value her by keeping my attention focused on her, even when I'm surrounded by a boisterous party full of diversions competing for my attention. This tells her that our relationship is important to me, that *she* is important to me and that when I promise to keep her in my prayers I mean to do it.

Our Best Time

In the course of a day it is easy to get so caught up in bouncing from one urgent crisis to the next that we never make time for the one relationship that, above all others, deserves our highest quality time: our relationship with God. We've said it before, but it bears repeating here: The Lord comes to us with a still, small voice, speaking most often not in a booming *basso profundo* that supercedes the boisterous events of life, but in a soothing tone audible most clearly only in the quiet downtimes of our lives. The question becomes: Do we value our privilege of relationship with the Creator of the universe enough to carve out focused time for Him despite or amid the busyness of our lives?

I've always loved the word picture the apostle John records for us in Revelation 3:20. He quotes Jesus, the undisputed and eternal ruler of the universe, as saying, "Here I am! I stand at the door and knock. If anyone hears my voice and opens the door, I will come in and eat with him, and he with me." Not, "Here I am pounding on the door and demanding my rightful entrance." Rather, "Here I am standing at the door, waiting for you to invite me in." He will only knock quietly and tenderly, seeking our company but not requiring it.

It is relevant to note that although this verse is often used in salvation explanations to lead people to invite Jesus into their lives and forgive their sins, it was originally spoken not to the lost but to His followers in the church of Laodicea. It is not only the lost whom Jesus seeks, but also those of us who have let His voice be drowned out by the concerns of this world. He keeps on knocking for those of us who have allowed His companionship to be exchanged for our work, our play, even our families' needs.

Jesus, in His very nature a member of the Godhead who was never separated from His Father's voice (except for the brief moment on the cross that split history in two), required focused time alone in conversation with His Father (see Luke 9:28 and John 6:15 for two examples). How much more, then, do we who tend to be disconnected from the holy God by our rebellious human natures need to make a priority of spending quality time focused on listening to His voice and getting to know Him?

He won't scream for our attention, so we need to set for ourselves frequent reminders not to ignore His gentle voice. Here are three reminders that have worked well for me:

- A formal appointment listed on my daily calendar.
- An open Bible on a desk I pass frequently.
- A worship CD that goes on as soon as I start my car.

In the Final Analysis

What's more important to file in the annals of today: a child's first rainbow or a perfectly orchestrated dinner party? the music program at church or the opportunity to lead a child to Christ? Do we spend an hour gossiping with a friend on the telephone or surfing the web, or prayerfully reading God's Word to receive guidance, comfort and correction? Do we plan a restful retreat with our fishing poles and our Bibles at a cabin in Canada or spend the weekend in a semi-darkened office buried beneath piles of paperwork?

Remember Kurt and Pam in the car with their son? Kurt chose to listen to the still voice of God. He stopped what he was doing and asked, "Ethan, do you know what it means to be saved?" Ethan initially answered yes, but then he got serious and changed his answer to no, but indicated an interest in knowing more. So, between placing their drive-thru order and picking it up at the second window, Kurt and Pam explained the gift of salvation to their young son. Right there in the drive-thru lane, Ethan decided to pray and ask Jesus to forgive him of his sins. (Pam prayed simultaneously that the drive-thru guys would take their time and not interrupt such an important eternity moment.) Kurt and Pam made the right call.

Oh, and remember the little girl, the dinner party and the rainbow? As I am the girl, I remember the choice my mom made. She turned off the stove and shared the rainbow with me. She chose the important—me—over the urgent—her guests' palates. Isn't it interesting that I still remember the choice my mother made, more than thirty years later?

Challenge of the Week

Take some focused time to compare Jesus' clipped and sometimes angry responses to the horde of questioning Pharisees in John 8 with His extended and truth-packed conversation with the individual Pharisee Nicodemus in John 3. Read the passages carefully. Note possible reasons Jesus made the choices and responses He made. Then journal your thoughts on ways you can learn from Jesus' responses to balance the needs of the urgent with the needs of those truly important individuals and relationships in your life.

Myth: There is one set of priorities and one life pattern
that every person must follow.

One Sunday morning about five years ago I arrived at church early—really early. I always arrived before most people because I was the designated alto on the worship team, and our rehearsal began a half hour before Sunday school. (As soon as rehearsal was over and we'd finished praying together, I'd dash off to the single adult Sunday school class I co-taught, then I was on to choir practice, then the worship service, then off to lunch with the singles. All in all, I felt pretty important to God on Sunday mornings—what with all the work I did for Him.)

This particular Sunday I arrived early even for me. So, I sat in the shadows at the back of the sanctuary (under the balcony) and watched as a hive of activity went on around me. Prior to that day I had been intimately familiar with the up-front players with whom I shared a platform every Sunday worship service—the worship team, the choir, the instrumentalists, the song leaders, the preacher, the soloists; I'd even been duly grateful for the diligence of the sound technicians, ushers and lighting guys. But I was completely unaware that there is another crew of quiet servants, just as crucial to the ongoing life of the church. As these servants worked that morning, I observed in silent amazement.

- I saw my friend Lisa's father, Bob, drag a two-story ladder from its storage closet and lumber up its rungs to change the lightbulb over the organ, which had burned out since the Wednesday night service.

- I saw Vince and his wife Nancy—they had already been at the church for at least an hour that morning—filling tray upon tray of tiny communion cups with grape juice. I only observed the final act in this drama, as they gingerly carried the filled trays (with white-gloved hands) to the front of the sanctuary.

- I had also seen the church custodian before I entered the church. He was shoveling snow off the sidewalks and lugging twenty-pound bags of salt behind him to sprinkle on the freshly cleared walks.

- I saw at least a half dozen others: adjusting the temperature throughout the building, folding worship bulletins, setting up tables for the youth group's fund raiser, carrying in newly laundered bedding for the nursery cribs and the list goes on.

I had just been witness to some of the most beautiful sights in all of the earth, yet I hadn't seen the important contribution of others of God's chosen servants. There were many older saints whose faithful prayers down through the years had built that church in the first place. Many of them couldn't arrive early any longer (or even arrive at all on an icy January morning), but that didn't mean they were not still behind the scenes, interceding in prayer for the pastor and the congregation from stark rooms at the retirement home or even from hospital beds.

All of these individuals offered up their acts of service to the Lord (that day, as every other day) in as genuine and loving a way as those we all see at the front of the platform during the worship hour. Yet their works are largely hidden from view and too often are thankless. Are these works of less value to the kingdom of God than the talents of the up-front people? Certainly not. Someone has to pour the juice if the congregation is to share the sacrament of communion together. If someone doesn't change the lightbulb over the organ, the whole congregation is liable to recognize a few sour notes played by a musician whose hymnal is shrouded in darkness. And I shudder to think of the odor that would waft all the way into the sanctuary if someone didn't wash the linens dirtied the previous week by infants in the nursery.

Listen to the words penned by the apostle Paul nearly two millennia ago:

> If the whole body were an eye, where would the sense of hearing be? If the whole body were an ear, where would the sense of smell be? But in fact God has arranged the parts in the body, every one of them, just as he wanted them to be. If they were all one part, where would the body be? As it is, there are many parts, but one body.
>
> The eye cannot say to the hand, "I don't need you!" And the head cannot say to the feet, "I don't need you!". . . But God has combined the members of the body and has given greater honor to the parts that lacked it, so that there should be no division in the body, but that its parts should have equal concern for each other. If one part suffers, every part suffers with it; if one part is honored, every part rejoices with it.
>
> Now you are the body of Christ, and each one of you is a part of it. (1 Corinthians 12:17-21, 24-27)

If the Whole Body Were a Helping Hand

Why in a book on managing our use of time are we examining the concept of the various gifts and purposes God has established for those of us who are part of His body? It's perfectly logical, if you think about it. Allow me to tell you one more story, then I promise to explain the connection.

When I was growing up my mom had a wonderful friend, a godly woman who was diligent and infectious in her ministry-oriented fervor. She had a special gift for identifying hurting, lonely people and then offering her time and service in ministry to them. This was her calling. Her weeks included regularly scheduled visits to nursing homes and frequent care for shut-ins who didn't have family nearby.

My mom is also a tremendously gifted individual. During that season of her life, she was the Sunday morning organist at our church, the sole "low alto" in a traveling gospel singing group that rehearsed one day every week, a valued choir member, the pianist for a monthly luncheon of Christian women and also for a Bible study of 100 women who met every Tuesday morning, piano teacher to seven students ages three to twelve, to say nothing of the time she spent being an example to me of a Christ-centered homemaker, mother and wife. Those are the ways God used her most powerfully.

He always equips someone to do the tasks that need to be done—to clear the time and invest the resources to finish the work.

That said, though, Mom often felt inferior when she was with this friend. It was usually unspoken, but she would experience guilt for not sharing her friend's burden for sick elderly people. When her friend would ask Mom to accompany her on these missions of mercy, Mom would feel compelled to go. But when she'd return home, my mom would feel discouraged and drained from what she'd witnessed (rather like I felt years later after teaching third-grade Sunday school), because my mom's gifts are different than her friend's.

Was it wrong for my mom's friend to use her gifts in meeting the day-to-day needs of hurting people? Of course not. But it wouldn't be right for her to burden others (who are gifted in other areas) to fulfill her calling—this would, in fact, siphon time and energies away from the fulfillment of their individual callings. God doesn't require everyone to visit the nursing home. Just like He doesn't equip everyone to play the organ for the Sunday morning service, nor does He call everyone to teach Sunday school or climb a ladder to change a lightbulb or launder dirty linens for the nursery. But He always equips someone to do the tasks that need to be done—and whomever He calls and equips, it is that person who is responsible to fulfill the calling—to clear the time and invest the resources to finish the work.

So then, we come full circle back to that pesky element of time, of making difficult choices in order to use our resources most efficiently in God's service.

Nothing So Sacred About Mornings . . . or Evenings

Think back to the title of this chapter and to its accompanying myth. "You Have to Be a Morning Person" and "There is one set of priorities and one life pattern that every person must follow." My mom bought into this myth when she assumed that in order to be as spiritual and in touch with God as her friend was, she had to take on her friend's burden.

And there's a special reason for this chapter's title—*I* am not a morning person. Anyone who knows me at all will vouch for that statement's veracity. I recently saw a nightshirt that expresses my sentiment about any time before noon; it features a sleeping kitty and the caption "I don't DO mornings."

So, it frustrates me when people who *are* morning people insist that to be totally spiritual I need to rise at 4 a.m. to have my devotions and pray. Let me tell you, I've tried to force myself into that mold. Even with a double shot of espresso coursing through my veins, I am incoherent at 4 a.m., or even 6 a.m., for that matter. Early morning is not the prime time of my day to spend in communion with anyone, much less the God whose companionship I love. I'm pretty sure God knows this about me—He made me this way.

The fact is, God didn't create one mold for every individual to squeeze into.

So now when people remind me that Jesus rose early to pray (Mark 1:35), I remind them that He also stayed up late to do the same (Luke 6:12). In fact, to the really adamant morning people (you know who you are), I point out that Jesus never chastised anyone for failing to get up early to pray, but He did reprimand the disciples in the Garden of Gethsemane who failed to stay up late to pray with Him (Mark 14:37-38). Even in this area of our time usage, Jesus proved that He understands us just as we are.

The fact is, God didn't create one mold for every individual to squeeze into. He didn't create 6 billion morning people. He created us all colors, all shapes, with all different gifts and preferences and motivators. No one is superior, neither is anyone inferior. Yes, there is only one way to reach God in the first place (through the blood Jesus shed for the forgiveness of our sins; see John 14:6), but that's where the similarity ends. It's when we try to construe unity (which I would define as mutual respect lived out in everyday life) to mean unanimity (my definition: everyone has to be exactly the same) that we get ourselves and others into a sticky jam. It's when we're trying to do

someone else's work—whether because it seems more glamor-
ous, more spiritual or more important—(or when we're trying
to make someone else do our work) that we make the worst
time usage choices for our lives.

The Nature and Use of Gifts

The passage from First Corinthians that I quoted earlier
(about the body of Christ having many different members) is
one of many New Testament discussions of the gifts God's
Spirit bestows on individual believers. The apostle Peter adds
this insight to the subject when he writes,

> Each one should use whatever gift he has received to serve
> others, faithfully administering God's grace in its various
> forms. If anyone speaks, he should do it as one speaking the
> very words of God. If anyone serves, he should do it with
> the strength God provides, so that in all things God may be
> praised through Jesus Christ. To him be the glory and the
> power for ever and ever. Amen. (1 Peter 4:10-11)

Similarly, to the Romans Paul writes,

> We have different gifts, according to the grace given us. If a
> man's gift is prophesying, let him use it in proportion to his
> faith. If it is serving, let him serve; if it is teaching, let him
> teach; if it is encouraging, let him encourage; if it is contrib-
> uting to the needs of others, let him give generously; if it is
> leadership, let him govern diligently; if it is showing mercy,
> let him do it cheerfully. (Romans 12:6-8)

In all of these passages, I hear a three-pronged common refrain: 1) God gives gifts to His servants; 2) He gives these in variety for the benefit of His family; 3) He expects each recipient
to use these gifts willingly, joyfully and unselfishly for the purpose for which they are intended.

These truths are indivisibly intertwined with our time usage choices. Knowing how God has gifted—or has wired—me has provided me with an infallible litmus test as I set my priorities and make choices about what is included and what is excluded from my day planner each week.

My challenge to you is no different than the one I've issued to myself: Take the time and effort to discover the way God wired you. Once you have discerned this, put all your efforts into developing and nurturing those gifts so you can use them most efficiently for the benefit of Christ and His kingdom.

Whatever task it is that God has created for each of us, we are responsible to do it diligently, wholeheartedly and with an attitude of service to the God we love.

This could mean that you schedule your quiet times with God in the midday, afternoon or evening, because you're like I am—definitely not a morning person. Or it could mean that you realize your gifting is similar to my mom's friend—in compassionate service to hurting people. So, you might ask your pastor for the name of an ailing church member who might enjoy a visit one afternoon this week. Or, if you realize your gift is in giving of your financial resources, you might schedule some time to research worthy ministries that would benefit from a donation. Or, if you realize your gift is teaching, you might clear your schedule one night a week to enroll in a class at the community college to study the learning patterns of children or adults.

Whatever task it is that God has created for each of us, we are responsible to do it diligently, wholeheartedly and with an attitude of service to the God we love. It is worth every ounce of expenditure of time and energy. Why? Let me close this chapter with some apropos words from Jesus that I believe offer a fitting answer:

> Then the righteous will answer him, "Lord, when did we see you hungry and feed you, or thirsty and give you something to drink? When did we see you a stranger and invite you in, or needing clothes and clothe you? When did we see you sick or in prison and go to visit you?"
>
> The King will reply, "I tell you the truth, whatever you did for one of the least of these brothers of mine, you did for me." (Matthew 25:37-40)

Challenge of the Week

Search your study Bible or other Bible reference book for all mentions on the subject of spiritual gifts. (I've found the *International Standard Bible Encyclopedia* to be a good reference resource.) You might want to begin by reading the passages quoted in this chapter in their complete context. Prayerfully read the descriptions of these gifts and ask the Lord to make clear to you the gift or gifts that He has given to you. Then search for ways to use those gifts—or to nurture and develop them—to benefit God's kingdom.

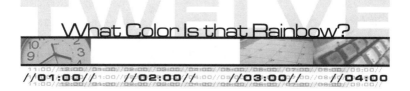
Myth: True efficiency means I'm being wasteful of time
or resources if I'm enjoying myself.

As I mentioned earlier, our family has spent the last year building onto and remodeling our home. To save money, we've taken on the task of purchasing and bringing home the various fixtures (lighting, closet organizers, vanities, countertops, small built-in items, wood planks, forty-five boxes of floor tile, etc.) necessary for the finishing work. Of our three cars, mine is most efficient for carrying planks, closet organizers and sundry large items because the back seat folds out of the way and doubles the length of the trunk.

Now, my mom is normally the driver in the family. She actually likes being behind the wheel. I, on the other hand, drive only out of necessity. (Perhaps my ambivalence is rooted in my many years as a rush-hour commuter.) But, because my car is perfect for transporting large items, lately I've been doing more of the driving and mom has been doing more of the sitting.

The other day as I drove to the home improvement store, Mom commented about the colorfully manicured landscaping of a home we pass frequently. I'd noticed it maybe a hundred trips ago, but Mom, normally more intent on driving than sightseeing, excitedly noticed it for the very first time. Later, it occurred to me that because someone else was shouldering part of the burden, Mom was able to seize a refreshing moment to enjoy the journey and to notice beauty along the way.

Some People Sap Creativity

I have found that a well-managed, well-ordered life is one marked by joyous discoveries like the one Mom made that afternoon. It is not always filled with happiness (we do live in a world marred by sin), but a constant source of joy is never far away, if we make the effort to seek it out. I'd define that joy as the inner fulfillment that flows from finding the best ways to expend our energies. Joy, for me, is having the privilege of accomplishing my life-mission with finesse and panache and a healthy dash of pizzazz.

> I have found that a well-managed, well-ordered life is one marked by joyous discoveries.

Not everyone takes the time to notice beauty or experience joy, though, even when it is right before their eyes. I had a boss a few years back who lived as though beauty were one great big waste of time, and he was forever on the hunt for converts to his way of approaching life.

Let me preface my comments by noting that creative people are difficult to manage. I know, because I am one. And I have managed whole departments of people who are similarly inclined. We operate on a different wavelength than most number crunchers, efficiency experts and MBAs. Give us a deadline and we'll meet it, but not in a nine-to-five setting.

I'll actually be working even when I don't look like I'm working: in the shower, while scrubbing the tub, while lying in bed. Now, I'm not talking about waiting for some nebulous creative muse to show up and inspire me. Rather, I mean that creativity happens in the mind before it happens on paper. Because of this, I generally do some of my best work when I am relaxed, comfortable, at peace and wrapped up in my cuddly quilt at 2 a.m.

This particular boss was driven—an efficiency fanatic to the extreme. He believed efficiency was a matter of spending every moment in frenetic activity. His theory was: you produce measurable work from the moment you walk in the door at 7 a.m. until you leave at 5 p.m., then you produce more work while you're commuting home, then you go home for a few hours and come back to produce work again. He had contempt for the intangible processes necessary to creativity such as bouncing ideas off colleagues, brainstorming and thinking before committing something to paper.

While I met every deadline he established for me and achieved every work-related goal he set, I was frequently subject to his fury when he would walk into my office and find me staring out the window or gazing absently into a blank computer screen. What he couldn't see was that beneath the staring or gazing I was processing, creating and prewriting. I was working, but it wasn't tangible so it didn't fit his expectations.

This boss sapped the creativity—and the joy—right out of me. He couldn't tolerate the idea of "wasting" time to look for joy along the way, and he wouldn't stand for any of us to seek joy, either. Under his tutelage, the writing journey was harsh, cruel and inflexible—and the end product lacked the luster and panache that flow from a joyful heart.

The Case for Enjoyment

Like this boss, many of us have been conditioned with a rigid view of God's expectations. We live in a culture that sees God as a kill-joy, a cruel taskmaster who would begrudge us every opportunity to do something fun. Nose to the grindstone. Work, work, work. No looking about or dawdling.

Does this view of our heavenly Father accurately portray the picture Jesus painted when He described the life He offers us as "abundant"? It is my contention that rather than being extraneous wastes of time, joy and beauty are elements of God's good creation meant to be noticed, appreciated and even celebrated.

The God I see revealed in the pages of the Bible loved a good party. Early in the Old Testament He established times and seasons for His people to celebrate: Sabbaths once a week to celebrate God's faithfulness, periodic feasts, annual festivals. In fact, there was a whole year (one in every fifty) called *Jubilee*. God didn't tell the people, "If you have time and aren't too busy with your work herding flocks or harvesting wheat, why don't you take a minute to celebrate." Festivals, feasts and parties— some that lasted an entire week or longer—were integral parts of God's law. Observance was not optional, it was mandatory, and resistance was a great offense.

> Rather than being extraneous wastes of time,
> joy and beauty are elements of God's
> good creation meant to be noticed,
> appreciated and even celebrated.

I began to wonder, as I read through the list of feasts and celebrations on the Hebrew calendar, why God had established those times. One reason is likely to have been something we discussed earlier: namely, the fact that the human body requires rest and refreshment. But, I think the celebrations went deeper than just the physical necessity of rest. I think they were a reflection of a portion of God's character. In Genesis 1-2 we can observe that when He formed each element of creation, He celebrated the fact that it was good. He enjoyed examining the fruits of His creativity. I don't think He rested on the seventh day because He was tired (according to Isaiah 40:28, He doesn't get tired or grow weary like we do). I think God rested so He could lean over the portal of heaven, survey all of creation and enjoy the view.

It's Party Time

There is yet another reason I believe God wove celebrations into the fabric of His people's lives: Stepping back and throwing a party would cause them to remember how faithful He had been in the past and would encourage them not to grow weary of life's daily struggles.

Five years ago I latched on to this idea of celebration and added it to my time management repertoire. I was, at the time, writing my first book. As I set my writing schedule, I quickly recognized that it would be exhausting and potentially draining—not because I wouldn't enjoy the subject matter or the process, but because it was just one on top of many other projects that required my time and energies.

So, I did some calculations: When should I have the research completed? When should I reach the halfway point of writing the first draft? When should I have the first draft completed? When should I have the project printed out and ready to proofread? I put those target dates on the calendar and shared them with my accountability partner.

As each target approached and I met that interim deadline, my accountability partner and I would hold a little celebration—we'd go out to lunch or dinner or take a few hours to browse at the mall. When I completed the first draft, in fact, she placed a small congratulatory gift in my hand as a memento of the achievement. These celebrations did more than provide a needed refreshment or diversion: They reminded me to recognize God's provision all along the way, and they allowed me to appreciate the opportunities He was giving me to use my gifts to bring Him glory.

Jesus Liked a Good Party

But we're New Testament people, you might say, no longer subject to the Old Testament rules and regulations. OK, I'll buy that. But look at Jesus: throngs of children flocked to sit on His lap; throngs of adults set aside their daily agendas to hang on His every word. And He was known to fraternize—party, even—with brides and grooms and IRS guys (well, tax collectors).

Let me ask you: Do kids fight to sit on the laps of cold, disinterested people who are too busy, too self-important or too focused on efficiency to notice them? Do brides and grooms choose dour and dull guys to invite to their weddings? Do crowds of everyday people find themselves drawn to a staid, drab or dictatorial individual? No! People look for someone vibrant, someone with charisma, someone oozing with contagious energy. And that's just how Jesus spent His earthly ministry. He was colorful and magnetic. He was the epitome of joy. Yes, He was focused on His task; yes, He was clear about His objectives. But He made life interesting (never a dull moment with Him); He was the center of the party; He made life . . . alive.

Joy in the Journey

How does this play out in everyday life?

I had lunch yesterday with a friend (in fact, another former boss) who has found joy in his retirement season. A former pastor and editor, Don is now working hour after hour every day of his retirement by tutoring foreign students in English as a second language. His eyes light up as he talks about the progress of his students, and he is overjoyed when in addition to reading and writing, his students ask him to teach them about his God. You don't have to know Don well to recognize by the look on his face and the lilt in his voice that he has found joy in the journey.

Another friend, Lin, travels the country teaching wanna-be writers how to navigate the writing life. A former Christian education professor, Lin combines all of her talents and gifts in this vocation. She racks up flying miles faster than some pilots I know. Every time I talk with her, she is just home from one trip or just packing for another. In an unlikely combination, Lin's other passion is roller coasters. On many trips she finds time to add a day or two to visit a nearby amusement park and ride its largest coaster. She travels for her work but also seizes the opportunities the work creates for her to experience great enjoyment.

Let's say "yes" by adding to our daily agendas those things that God has created for us to accomplish, and let's say "yes" to meeting each appointment with godly joy and enthusiasm.

I could list dozens of other everyday folks who are productive and yet enjoying the journey—the single man who uses his talents as a recreational director for inner-city youth, the engineer who enjoys oil painting in his off hours, the soccer mom who is enrolled in a pottery course at the community college. I've tried to work both ways—with inflexible efficiency and with joyful productivity—and I'd choose the latter every time.

Truthful Time Factors

As I've been considering this whole idea of joy in life's journey, it occurs to me that it just may be time for us to toss out the myths that have been holding us back and replace them with their joyfully positive counterparts. So, out with the old and in with the new. I think this new list will meet our needs quite well:

1. I will say yes to those things that fit clearly and comfortably into my God-given objectives.
2. I will operate each day with the knowledge that ultimately I answer to God, and God alone, for the way I've chosen to use those hours, days and years He has given me.
3. I will intentionally and regularly schedule "time-outs" with God to enhance my spiritual maturation.
4. I will use every scrap and slice of time to its fullest in meeting my life's goals and objectives.
5. I will feel no guilt when I manage daily interruptions that would seek to sidetrack me from achieving the purpose God has for me.
6. I will actively seek out a trustworthy accountability partner to help keep me motivated and on track.
7. I will entrust to God's care the needs of each person in my life while I do what is within my power to nurture and encourage them in the fulfillment of their dreams.
8. I will recognize and be grateful for the inherent limitations of the season of life I'm currently experiencing.
9. I will confidently schedule "time-outs" for my own physical rejuvenation.
10. I will seize poignant, teachable moments with those I love and make them a priority—even over some of the urgent tasks that scream for my attention.
11. I will relish the uniqueness God has placed in me and appreciate the uniqueness He has placed in other people.
12. I will take every opportunity to celebrate and enjoy to the fullest the pursuit of those tasks that God has created for me to accomplish.

Well, then, let's not waste another moment. Let's say "yes" by adding to our daily agendas those things that God has created for us to accomplish, and let's say "yes" to meeting each appointment with godly joy and enthusiasm.

I hope to meet up with you along the journey so we can celebrate together. If not, I'll see you when we all get home, and I can assure you that's going to be one awesome party.

Challenge of the Week

Search the Bible—both Old and New Testaments—for evidence of parties, celebrations and festivals. Pay special attention to the end-of-time party being planned in heaven to welcome God's children home. Note the elements common to all of these events. Then schedule your own interim celebrations to enjoy and appreciate the bountiful gifts God has entrusted to you.

Addendum
Periodic
Self-Assessment Quiz

Is my schedule running me? How can I take control if it is?

_____

_____

_____

_____

_____

Is my life in balance? If not, how can I begin to move toward
balancing it? _____

_____

_____

_____

To whom can I look for a living, breathing example of a balanced,
godly life? _____

_____

_____

_____

_____

What areas of my life *can* I control that I'm not controlling now?

_____

_____

_____

_____

What have I done in the last month that moves me toward accomplishing my life's goals?

_____

_____

_____

_____

If I've gotten off track, how can I begin to initiate a correction?

_____

_____

_____

_____

What elements of my life deserve more time than I've been
giving them? _____

_____

_____

_____

_____

What elements of my life deserve less time in my schedule?

_____

_____

_____

_____

Will diminishing them cause me to have to break some bad
habits? If so, here's how I'll do it: _____

_____

_____

_____

_____

Do I have a trusted advisor who will give me loving, honest input and who will hold me accountable to stay true to the goals and objectives I've set?

_____

_____

_____

_____

Do I have a practical, easy-to-use system that I use to record all the important agenda and lifestyle items in my life? Am I using that system to the fullest or are there more ways I can adapt it to serve me better as my "trusted assistant" in conquering my time factor?

_____

_____

_____

_____

_____

If we may assist you in knowing more about Jesus Christ and the Christian life, or if you would like to let the author know how this book has affected your life, please write us at:

Christian Publications, Inc.
Attention: Editorial Department
3825 Hartzdale Drive
Camp Hill, PA 17011